BETWEEN GRADES 3 & 4

Weekly Reader:
SUMMER EXPRESS

New York • Toronto • London • Auckland • Sydney
Mexico City • New Delhi • Hong Kong • Buenos Aires

Editor: Ourania Papacharalambous
Cover design by Tannaz Fassihi and Michelle H. Kim
Interior design by Michelle H. Kim

ISBN: 978-1-338-10892-7
Compilation and illustrations copyright © 2017 by Scholastic Inc.
All rights reserved.
Printed in the U.S.A.
First printing, January 2017.

10 11 12 13 14 15   144   25 24 23 22

Table of Contents

Dear Parent,

Congratulations! You hold in your hands an exceptional educational tool that will give your child a head start in the coming school year.

Inside this book, you'll find 100 practice pages that will help your child review and learn reading and writing skills, grammar, place value, addition and subtraction, multiplication and division, fractions, and so much more! *Weekly Reader: Summer Express* is divided into 10 weeks, with two practice pages for each day of the week, Monday through Friday. However, feel free to use the pages in any order that your child would like. Here are other features you'll find inside:

★ A weekly incentive chart and certificate to motivate and reward your child for his or her efforts.

★ A sheet of colorful stickers to use as weekly rewards.

★ Ideas for fun, skill-building activities you can do with your child any time.

★ Suggestions for creative learning activities that you can do with your child each week.

★ A certificate of completion to celebrate your child's accomplishments.

We hope you and your child will have a lot of fun as you work together to complete this workbook.

Enjoy!

The Editors

Tips for Using This Book

1. Pick a good time for your child to work on the activities. You may want to do it around mid-morning after play, or early afternoon when your child is not too tired.

2. Make sure your child has all the supplies he or she needs, such as pencils and an eraser. Designate a special place for your child to work.

3. Celebrate your child's accomplishments by letting him or her affix stickers to the incentive chart after completing the activities each day. Reward your child's efforts with a bonus sticker at the end of the week as well.

4. Encourage your child to complete the worksheets, but don't force the issue. While you may want to ensure that your child succeeds, it's also important that he or she maintains a positive and relaxed attitude toward school and learning.

5. After you've given your child a few minutes to look over the activity pages he or she will be working on, ask your child to tell you his or her plan of action: "Tell me about what we're doing on these pages." Hearing the explanation aloud can provide you with insights into your child's thinking processes. Can he or she complete the work independently? With guidance? If your child needs support, try offering a choice about which family member might help. Giving your child a choice can help boost confidence and help him or her feel more ownership of the work to be done.

6. When your child has finished the workbook, present him or her with the certificate of completion on page 143. Feel free to frame or laminate the certificate and display it on the wall for everyone to see. Your child will be so proud!

Skill-Building Activities for Any Time

The following activities are designed to complement the 10 weeks of practice pages in this book. These activities don't take more than a few minutes to complete and are just a handful of ways in which you can enrich and enliven your child's learning. Use the activities to take advantage of time you might ordinarily disregard—for example, standing in line or waiting at a bus stop. You'll be working to practice key skills and have fun together at the same time.

Find Real-Life Connections

One of the reasons for schooling is to help children function in the real world, to empower them with the abilities they'll truly need. So why not put those developing skills into action by enlisting your child's help with creating a grocery list, reading street signs, sorting pocket change, and so on? He or she can apply reading, writing, science, and math skills in important and practical ways, connecting what he or she is learning with everyday tasks.

An Eye for Patterns

A red-brick sidewalk, a beaded necklace, a Sunday newspaper—all show evidence of structure and organization. You can help your child recognize the way things are structured, or organized, by observing and talking about patterns they see. Your child will apply his or her developing ability to spot patterns across all school subject areas, including attributes of shapes and solids (geometry) and characteristics of narrative stories (reading). Being able to notice patterns is a skill shared by effective readers and writers, scientists, and mathematicians.

Journals as Learning Tools

Most of us associate journal writing with reading comprehension, but having your child keep a journal can help you keep up with his or her developing skills in other academic areas as well—from telling time to matching rhymes. To get started, provide your child with several sheets of paper, folded in half, and stapled together. Explain that he or she will be writing and/or drawing in the journal to complement the practice pages completed each week. Encourage your child to draw or write about what he or she found easy, what was difficult, or what was fun. Before moving on to another set of practice pages, take a few minutes to read and discuss that week's journal entries together.

Promote Reading at Home

- Let your child catch you in the act of reading for pleasure, whether you like reading science fiction novels or do-it-yourself magazines. Store them someplace that encourages you to read in front of your child and **demonstrate that reading is an activity you enjoy**. For example, locate your reading materials on the coffee table instead of your nightstand.

- Set aside a family reading time. By designating a reading time each week, your family is assured an opportunity to discuss with each other what you're reading. You can, for example, share a funny quote from an article. Or your child can tell you his or her favorite part of a story. The key is to **make a family tradition of reading and sharing books** of all kinds together.

- **Put together collections of reading materials** your child can access easily. Gather them in baskets or bins that you can place in the family room, the car, and your child's bedroom. You can refresh your child's library by borrowing materials from your community's library, buying used books, or swapping books and magazines with friends and neighbors.

Skills Alignment

Listed below are the skills covered in the activities throughout *Weekly Reader: Summer Express*. These skills will help children review what they know while helping prevent summer learning loss. They will also better prepare each child to meet, in the coming school year, the math and language arts learning standards established by educators.

Math

Skill	Week 1	Week 2	Week 3	Week 4	Week 5	Week 6	Week 7	Week 8	Week 9	Week 10
Represent and solve problems involving multiplication and division.	✦	✦	✦	✦	✦	✦	✦	✦	✦	✦
Understand properties of multiplication and the relationship between multiplication and division.		✦	✦	✦				✦	✦	
Multiply and divide within 100.	✦	✦	✦	✦	✦			✦	✦	
Solve problems involving the four operations and identify patterns.	✦	✦	✦	✦				✦		
Use place value understanding and properties of operations to perform multi-digit arithmetic.	✦					✦		✦		
Develop understanding of fractions as numbers.							✦	✦	✦	✦
Solve problems involving measurement and estimation of intervals of time, liquid volumes, and masses of objects.		✦			✦					
Represent and interpret data.							✦	✦		✦
Understand area and relate area to multiplication and to addition.						✦	✦	✦	✦	
Recognize perimeter as an attribute of plane figures and distinguish between linear and area measures.							✦	✦		✦	✦
Reason with shapes and their attributes.							✦	✦	✦	

Language Arts

Skill	Week 1	Week 2	Week 3	Week 4	Week 5	Week 6	Week 7	Week 8	Week 9	Week 10
Ask and answer questions about key details in a text.	✦	✦		✦		✦		✦		✦
Determine the central message, lesson, moral, or main idea of a text.		✦	✦	✦		✦		✦		
Describe characters and how their actions contribute to events in the story.				✦		✦		✦		
Describe connections between events, ideas, procedural steps in a text.							✦		✦	✦
Use text features and search tools to locate information in a text.					✦					
Distinguish own point of view from that of narrator, characters, or author.								✦		
Use images and words in a text to demonstrate understanding of the text.	✦					✦				
Compare and contrast two texts on similar topics or by the same author.								✦	✦	✦
Read and comprehend grade-appropriate texts.	✦	✦	✦	✦	✦	✦	✦	✦	✦	✦
Know and apply grade-level phonics and word analysis skills in decoding words.		✦					✦			
Write opinion pieces, informative/explanatory essays, and narratives.				✦			✦			✦
Use linking and temporal words and phrases in writing.				✦	✦					✦
Demonstrate command of standard English grammar and usage.	✦	✦	✦	✦		✦	✦	✦	✦	
Demonstrate command of standard English capitalization, punctuation, and spelling when writing.	✦	✦				✦				✦
Determine or clarify the meaning of unknown and multiple-meaning words and phrases.	✦		✦	✦	✦		✦			
Demonstrate understanding of figurative language, word relationships, and nuances in word meanings.				✦	✦	✦	✦	✦		

Help Your Child Get Ready: Week 1

Here are some activities that you and your child might enjoy.

Comic Order

Build up your child's sequencing skills. Cut a comic strip into sections. Ask your child to put the strip in the correct order and to explain his or her thinking.

Make a Time Capsule

Make a time capsule with your child. Ask him or her to think about what objects could be included in the capsule that will tell people in the future about your family and about the time period you live in. Put all the items in a container and bury it. (A metal container will work best.)

My Summer Plan

Suggest that your child come up with a plan to achieve a goal by the end of the summer. Help him or her map out a way to be successful. Periodically, check to see how he or she is progressing.

Listen and Draw

Describe an object, animal, or person to your child and ask him or her to draw it. How close does the drawing come to looking like the real thing? Then, ask him or her to describe something for you to draw.

These are the skills your child will be working on this week.

Math

- addition with and without regrouping
- multiply by 8s and 9s
- subtraction with regrouping
- round to the nearest 10
- determine an unknown factor

Reading

- reading comprehension

Phonics & Vocabulary

- use a dictionary

Grammar & Writing

- nouns
- adjectives
- capitalization and punctuation

Incentive Chart: Week 1

Week 1	Day 1	Day 2	Day 3	Day 4	Day 5
Put a sticker to show you completed each day's work.	☆ ☆	☆ ☆	☆ ☆	☆ ☆	☆ ☆

CONGRATULATIONS!

Wow! You did a great job this week!

This certificate is presented to:

_____

_____   _____
Date   Parent/Caregiver's Signature

Help Your Child Get Ready: Week 2

Here are some activities that you and your child might enjoy.

Newspaper Treasure Hunt

In this special hunt, your child looks for various "treasures" in a newspaper article. The treasures are letters or symbols to which you've assigned a value. For example, a *Z* might be worth $10 and an exclamation point might be worth $5. Have your child search an article to find out how valuable its "treasure" is.

Two-Minute Lists

Give your child two minutes to list as many words as he or she can think of that include double letters.

What's in a Name?

Have your child research his or her name. Have him or her find out what the name means. Then tell your child the story of how you chose it. Encourage him or her to find out the meanings of other family members' names as well.

Leaf Survey

What kinds of leaves are in your neighborhood? Have your child do a leaf survey. He or she can collect leaves, use reference books to identify them, and then make a list of all the different trees found in your area.

These are the skills your child will be working on this week.

Math

- identify arithmetic patterns
- identify missing dividends
- division
- measure and estimate volume and mass

Reading

- main idea and details

Phonics & Vocabulary

- spelling

Grammar & Writing

- comparative and superlative adjectives
- personal pronouns
- punctuation: statements, questions, exclamations

Incentive Chart: Week 2

Week 2	Day 1	Day 2	Day 3	Day 4	Day 5
Put a sticker to show you completed each day's work.	☆ ☆	☆ ☆	☆ ☆	☆ ☆	☆ ☆

CONGRATULATIONS!

Wow! You did a great job this week!

This certificate is presented to:

_____

_____   _____
Date   Parent/Caregiver's Signature

Help Your Child Get Ready: Week 3

Here are some activities that you and your child might enjoy.

Start Collecting

Having a collection is a great way for a child to develop higher-level thinking skills like sorting and analyzing. Encourage your child to start one. Leaves, rocks, stamps, or shells are all easy and fun things to collect.

Invent a Board Game

With a few pieces of cardboard and some colored markers, your child can create his or her own board game. To start, suggest he or she model the game on any popular board game. The game might have a special theme, such as knights or dinosaurs. Be sure he or she writes out directions for the game. Then play a round!

Flash Card Facts

Have your child create his or her own set of multiplication facts flash cards. Then use them on a regular basis to help keep computation skills sharp.

Menu Planner

With your child, decide on a healthy eating style for the whole family. For guidance, locate the Dietary Guidelines for Americans published by the USDA or go to the ChooseMyPlate.gov website. Then, ask your child to plan the family's dinner menu for the week based on your chosen healthy eating style.

These are the skills your child will be working on this week.

Math

- multiply within 100
- use arrays
- determine an unknown factor

Reading

- identify problem and solution

Phonics & Vocabulary

- prefixes: *mis-, in-, sub-, un-, re-*
- develop vocabulary

Grammar & Writing

- irregular plurals
- build a paragraph: topic sentences

Incentive Chart: Week 3

Week 3	Day 1	Day 2	Day 3	Day 4	Day 5
Put a sticker to show you completed each day's work.	☆ ☆	☆ ☆	☆ ☆	☆ ☆	☆ ☆

CONGRATULATIONS!

Wow! You did a great job this week!

This certificate is presented to:

_____

_____ _____
Date   Parent/Caregiver's Signature

Help Your Child Get Ready: Week 4

Here are some activities that you and your child might enjoy.

Compound It

Ask your child to see how many compound words he or she can list that contain a specific word, such as the word *life*. (*lifeboat*, *lifeguard*, *lifetime*)

ABC Order

Read a list of eight to ten words to your child. Then have him or her put the words in alphabetical order.

Weather Watch

Have your child track the weather for a week. He or she can record the temperature and precipitation each day on a chart. You might also have him or her compare the weather forecast to the actual weather.

Idiom Illustrations

Help your child develop an understanding of idioms by asking him or her to illustrate a few. Some examples are: "have your cake and eat it too," "out of the frying pan and into the fire," "smell a rat," "rock the boat," "have egg on your face," and "let the cat out of the bag."

These are the skills your child will be working on this week.

Math
- multiply and divide within 100
- identify fact families
- commutative properties of multiplication
- division without remainders

Reading
- text features
- author's purpose

Phonics & Vocabulary
- root words
- synonyms
- antonyms
- homophones

Grammar & Writing
- plural nouns
- conjunctions

Let the cat out of the bag

Incentive Chart: Week 4

Week 4	Day 1	Day 2	Day 3	Day 4	Day 5
Put a sticker to show you completed each day's work.	☆ ☆	☆ ☆	☆ ☆	☆ ☆	☆ ☆

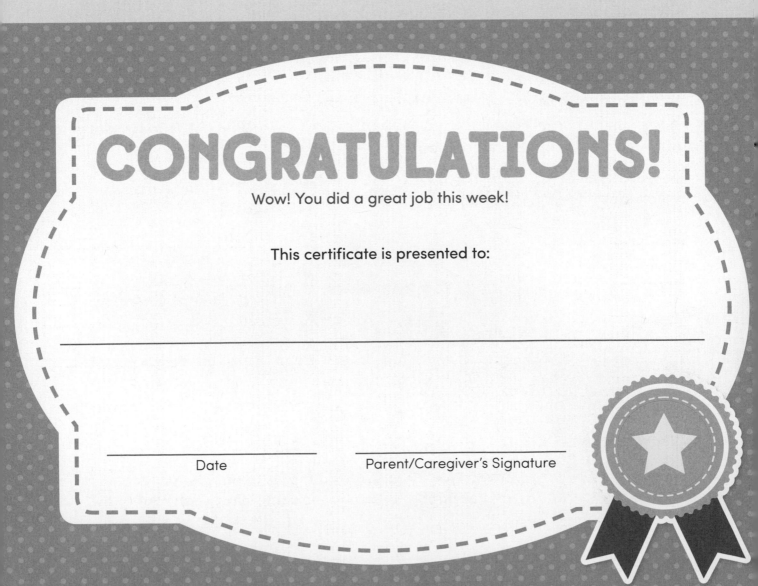

CONGRATULATIONS!

Wow! You did a great job this week!

This certificate is presented to:

_____

_____   _____

Date   Parent/Caregiver's Signature

The Root of the Matter

A word can have different parts. Many words have a main part, or **root**. The root contains the basic meaning of the word. For example, *ped* is the root in the word *pedal*. The meaning of *ped* is "foot." Feet are used to push down on the pedals of a bicycle to cause it to move.

The root is missing from a word in each sentence below. Use context clues and the meaning of the roots in the box to figure out the missing word part. Then write it in the space to complete the word.

> **pos** = place   **phon** = sound   **photo** = light
>
> **port** = carry   **pop** = people

1 The _____ulation of our town is just over 20,000.

2 The orchestra will perform a sym_____y by Beethoven.

3 The _____ition of the hour hand shows that it is 2:00 P.M.

4 What goods does our country ex_____ to other countries?

5 During _____synthesis, plants use sunlight to make food.

List the words you completed. Then write your own definition for each word. Use a dictionary if you are not sure.

6 _____

7 _____

8 _____

9 _____

10 _____

Challenge

What other words do you know with the roots *ped, pos, phon, photo, port,* and *pop*? On another sheet of paper, write a word containing each root.

What gives milk, says "moo," and makes wishes come true?

Find the missing factor or dividend.
Solve the riddle using your answers below.

_____ x 2 = 22 D	$4\overline{)}^{\,5}$ E
_____ x 7 = 84 G	$2\overline{)}^{\,2}$ A
_____ x 4 = 36 H	$3\overline{)}^{\,6}$ N
_____ x 3 = 24 I	_____ ÷ 1 = 7 O
_____ x 2 = 10 M	_____ ÷ 4 = 12 Y
_____ x 3 = 18 R	_____ ÷ 1 = 3 T

Solve the Riddle!

Write the letter that goes with each number.

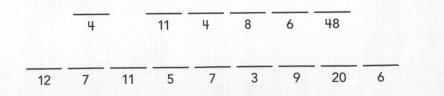

____   ____ ____ ____ ____ ____
4   11   4   8   6   48

____ ____ ____ ____ ____ ____ ____ ____ ____
12   7   11   5   7   3   9   20   6

The Case of the Bumbling Cupids

Big Boss Cupid wrote this memo to America's Cupids. But he's confused about plurals. Can you help?

For each pair of underlined words, circle the correctly spelled plural noun.

TO: America's Cupids
FROM: Big Boss Cupid

   This Valentine's Day, there will be 200 flying Cupids/Cupides around the skys/skies. You will be shooting your arrows/arrowes to bring love and happiness to lucky couples/couplese.

   Please be careful. A few years ago, a Cupid (who shall remain nameless) accidentally shot an elephant at the zoo, causing her to fall madly in love with one of the visitors. These kinds of terrible mistakes/mistaks give all of us a bad name. Do you know how long it took zookeepers to unwrap the elephant's trunk from around the poor visitor?

   We must avoid these disasters/disasteres in the future. Here are some tipps/tips to help you.

1. Practice your landings/landinges. Avoid slippery rooves/roofs. No one likes to see a Cupid falling into bushes/bushs or mailboxs/mailboxes.

2. Sharpen the points/pointes of your arrows. A dull arrow is likely to bounce right off your target.

3. Wear your glasses/glassess. If you can't see clearly, how can you be sure you're shooting the right person? Glasses also protect you from getting flys/flies in your eyes/eyies.

These simple rules will help make this the best holiday ever!

Family Fun

Multiplication is the opposite of division. The product and factors can be used to write division sentences. The multiplication and division sentences are called a **fact family**.

2 x 6 = 12 (2 groups of 6)   12 ÷ 6 = 2 (12 divided into 6 equal groups)

6 x 2 = 12 (6 groups of 2)   12 ÷ 2 = 6 (12 divided into 2 equal groups)

Write two multiplication and two division sentences for each set of numbers.

1 2, 3, 6

_____

_____

_____

_____

2 2, 8, 16

_____

_____

_____

_____

3 4, 5, 20

_____

_____

_____

_____

4 3, 5, 15

_____

_____

_____

_____

5 3, 9, 27

_____

_____

_____

_____

6 8, 5, 40

_____

_____

_____

_____

7 5, 6, 30

_____

_____

_____

_____

8 6, 7, 42

_____

_____

_____

_____

9 4, 8, 32

_____

_____

_____

_____

Challenge

Ramone has 33 marbles. He keeps an equal number of marbles in each of 3 bags. How many marbles are in each bag? On another sheet of paper, write a number sentence to solve this problem. Then write the set of numbers in this fact family.

A Perfect Match?

Each word in column 1 has a match in column 2. The match in column 2 is either a **synonym** (means the same thing, such as *right* and *correct*), **antonym** (means the opposite, such as *right* and *wrong*), or **homophone** (sounds the same, such as *right* and *write*).

Draw a line between each match and write which type of match it is. There is only one correct match for each word.

Column 1	Column 2	Type of Match
1. modern	**a.** exhausted	1 _____
2. sail	**b.** dusk	2 _____
3. thaw	**c.** gargantuan	3 _____
4. tired	**d.** late	4 _____
5. blue	**e.** ancient	5 _____
6. dawn	**f.** sale	6 _____
7. right	**g.** freeze	7 _____
8. minuscule	**h.** blew	8 _____
9. wear	**i.** dismantle	9 _____
10. tardy	**j.** great	10 _____
11. grate	**k.** live	11 _____
12. assemble	**l.** correct	12 _____
13. danger	**m.** hazard	13 _____
14. dwell	**n.** kernel	14 _____
15. colonel	**o.** where	15 _____

Change It Up

The order of the factors in a multiplication sentence can change without changing the value of the product. If *2 x 7* is changed to *7 x 2*, the product still equals *14*.

Change the order of the factors in each multiplication sentence.

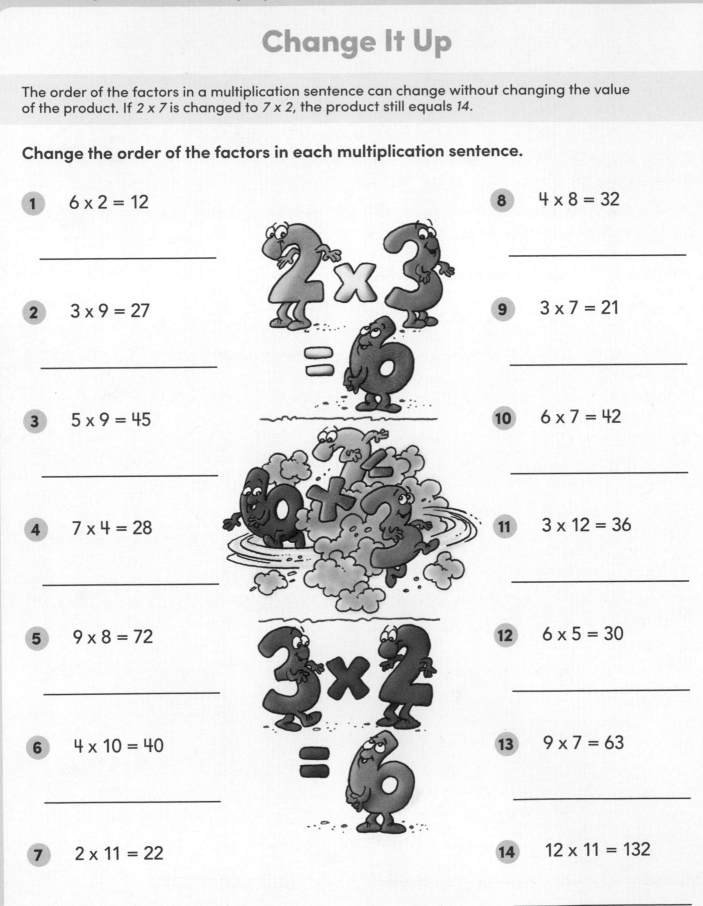

1 $6 \times 2 = 12$

_____

2 $3 \times 9 = 27$

_____

3 $5 \times 9 = 45$

_____

4 $7 \times 4 = 28$

_____

5 $9 \times 8 = 72$

_____

6 $4 \times 10 = 40$

_____

7 $2 \times 11 = 22$

_____

8 $4 \times 8 = 32$

_____

9 $3 \times 7 = 21$

_____

10 $6 \times 7 = 42$

_____

11 $3 \times 12 = 36$

_____

12 $6 \times 5 = 30$

_____

13 $9 \times 7 = 63$

_____

14 $12 \times 11 = 132$

_____

Glue Words

Conjunctions are words that join words or parts of sentences together. The most common conjunctions are *and, or,* and *but*. Each one means something different.

> *And* joins words or phrases that go together equally.
> *Or* gives you a choice.
> *But* introduces something that contrasts with something earlier in the sentence.

Write *and, or,* or *but* on the blank lines where you think they belong.

1 I completely forgot to study for the big math test, _____ amazingly, I still got all the answers right.

2 He saved his money for a whole year, _____ he bought himself a new bicycle.

3 "Either clean up your room this minute," her mother said, "_____ you're not going to the movies tonight!"

4 The weather was beautiful, _____ everyone loved the parade.

5 Would you like Italian _____ Chinese food for dinner?

6 Her face was dirty, her clothes were torn, and she was far from the palace, _____ I immediately knew she was the princess.

7 He was selected "Student of the Year" because he got the highest grades, was elected class president, _____ raised the most money in the charity marathon.

8 I don't have much money left, so I can buy either a pizza _____ my favorite magazine, but not both.

9 I memorized the whole script before the audition and acted my heart and soul out for the director, _____ I still didn't get a part in the play.

10 I can't decide which dog to adopt from the animal rescue league: the pretty Pomeranian _____ the dashing Dalmatian.

Keep On Dividing

Use these steps when dividing larger numbers.

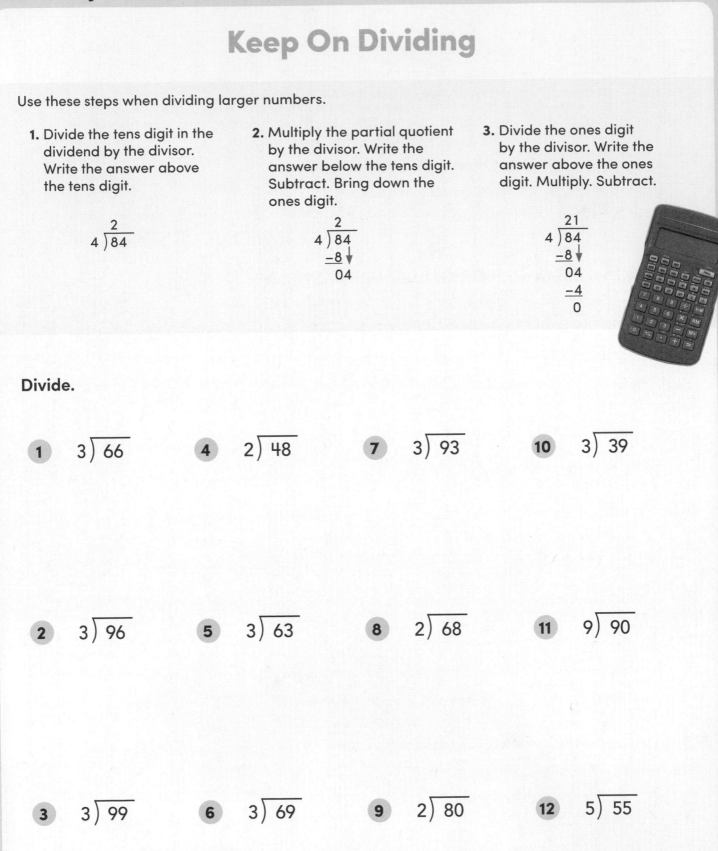

1. Divide the tens digit in the dividend by the divisor. Write the answer above the tens digit.

$$4\overline{)84}$$ with 2 above the tens digit

2. Multiply the partial quotient by the divisor. Write the answer below the tens digit. Subtract. Bring down the ones digit.

$$4\overline{)84}$$ with −8, 04

3. Divide the ones digit by the divisor. Write the answer above the ones digit. Multiply. Subtract.

$$4\overline{)84}$$ with 21 above, −8, 04, −4, 0

Divide.

1. $3\overline{)66}$

4. $2\overline{)48}$

7. $3\overline{)93}$

10. $3\overline{)39}$

2. $3\overline{)96}$

5. $3\overline{)63}$

8. $2\overline{)68}$

11. $9\overline{)90}$

3. $3\overline{)99}$

6. $3\overline{)69}$

9. $2\overline{)80}$

12. $5\overline{)55}$

A Rainforest Find

Read the article. Then answer the questions on page 56.

One night a few years ago, two scientists were exploring a rainforest in Costa Rica. Suddenly, they heard a loud buzzing noise. They shined their flashlights on the creature making the noise. It was a tiny frog!

The frog had huge white eyes and bright green coloring, like Kermit the Frog. It had other interesting features, too. For example, the skin on its belly was so clear that the scientists could see its insides.

Because it had clear skin, the scientists knew it was a type of glass frog (see sidebar). But they didn't recognize this type from their **research**. "We were excited," says scientist Brian Kubicki. "We had a feeling this was a species that was new to science."

In the Lab

Over time, the scientists found six of these frogs. They compared them with other glass frogs. They even used a computer to compare the noises the frogs made with the sounds of other frogs. The scientists proved that they had found a new **species**. They named it Diane's bare-hearted glass frog, after Kubicki's mom.

More to Learn

Finding a new species is not that unusual. Each year, scientists discover about 15,000 of them. Many are in rainforests and other spots that can be hard to explore.

Kubicki hopes to find other new **amphibians**. He says it's important to learn about all of Earth's animals. That way, people can help them and their habitats.

Glass Frogs

Frogs with clear or white skin on their bellies are known as glass frogs. The reason for the special skin is a mystery. There are 150 known species of glass frogs in the world.

Words to Know

research: the study of a subject

species: type of animal or plant

amphibians: animals that begin life in the water and move onto land as adults

A Rainforest Find (continued)

The glass frog shares its rainforest home with thousands of other species. This diagram shows the forest's four layers—and some creatures that live in each one.

Harpy eagle

Scarlet macaw

Spider monkey

Sloth

Red-eyed tree frog

Jaguar

Anaconda

Tapir

Layers of the Rainforest

The EMERGENT layer is where the tallest treetops stick out.

The CANOPY is where most of the treetops are. It's home to more types of animals than any other layer.

The UNDERSTORY gets little sunlight. Many plants here grow large leaves to soak up what sunlight they can.

The FOREST FLOOR is very shady and damp. A lot of insects live here.

Use the article and the diagram to answer the questions below.

1 The author's purpose in "A Rainforest Find" is to _____.
   ○ explain why many frogs live in rainforests
   ○ compare frogs with other amphibians
   ○ describe how scientists found a new species of frog
   ○ persuade readers to help save endangered frogs

2 In the article, the word *unusual* is used to mean _____.
   ○ common   ○ exciting   ○ uncommon   ○ important

3 According to the diagram, in which layer would you find the most animals?

   _____

4 The newly discovered glass frogs live in the understory. Name two other species that

   live in this layer. _____

5 The diagram shows two species that live in the emergent layer. What do they have in

   common? _____

Help Your Child Get Ready: Week 5

Here are some activities that you and your child might enjoy.

Homograph Duos

Ask your child to use each of the homographs *pen*, *uniform*, and *base* in two sentences that each show one of the word's meanings. For example, *Joe's pen was out of ink* and *The pigs ran out of the pen.*

What's Your Estimate

Ask your child to estimate how many times in 60 seconds he or she can say "Alabama" or touch his or her toes. Have him or her try the activity while you time it. Then compare the results with your child's estimate.

Order, Please!

Have your child put these time-period words in order from shortest to longest.

hour	week	millisecond
decade	day	minute

Tongue Twisters

Have fun with tongue twisters. See how many times your child can say a tongue twister in one minute. Here are some examples to get you started: "Some shun sunshine" and "How much wood would a wood chuck chuck if a wood chuck could chuck wood?"

These are the skills your child will be working on this week.

Math

- tell and write time
- understand area
- count square units
- use arrays

Reading

- analyze character

Phonics & Vocabulary

- similes
- metaphors

Grammar & Writing

- possessive pronouns
- verbs
- combine sentences

Incentive Chart: Week 5

Week 5	Day 1	Day 2	Day 3	Day 4	Day 5
Put a sticker to show you completed each day's work.	☆ ☆	☆ ☆	☆ ☆	☆ ☆	☆ ☆

CONGRATULATIONS!

Wow! You did a great job this week!

This certificate is presented to:

_____

_____   _____
Date   Parent/Caregiver's Signature

Possessive Pronouns

Possessive pronouns come before nouns and show ownership.
Some possessive pronouns are: *my, his, her, its, your, our,* and *their.*

For example: *Lisa has a pet frog. His name is Hopper.*
   His (possessive pronoun) takes the place of *frog* (noun).

Fill in the blanks with one of the possessive pronouns listed above.

1   The firemen showed _____ class how to climb a ladder.

2   Peter cleaned _____ room.

3   Kate loves to play soccer. _____ favorite position is goalie.

4   The students planned a surprise party for _____ teacher.

5   "Mrs. Ruiz, please take _____ students through the museum."

6   We celebrated _____ team's win against the visitors.

7   "_____ dog just had puppies," said Karen.

8   The boy thanked _____ teacher for helping him with his French homework.

9   Bobby, Joel, and Jack helped _____ coach put away the baseball equipment.

10   The spider spun _____ web near the door.

11   Julie came into the room and asked, "Why are _____ papers all over the floor?"

12   Why can't you put _____ things away neatly?

13   After Vernon saw the movie, he got into _____ car and drove away.

14   The girls said a few words and then put _____ coats on and went home.

15   _____ mom was so tired that we cooked dinner for her.

Time for Math

Fill in the circle for each correct answer.

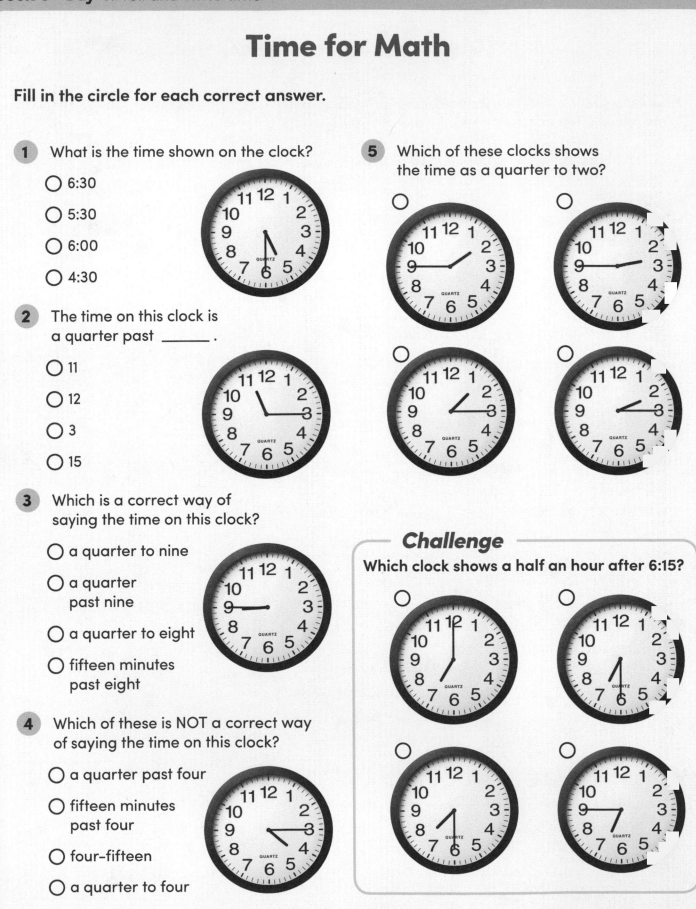

1 What is the time shown on the clock?

○ 6:30

○ 5:30

○ 6:00

○ 4:30

2 The time on this clock is a quarter past _____ .

○ 11

○ 12

○ 3

○ 15

3 Which is a correct way of saying the time on this clock?

○ a quarter to nine

○ a quarter past nine

○ a quarter to eight

○ fifteen minutes past eight

4 Which of these is NOT a correct way of saying the time on this clock?

○ a quarter past four

○ fifteen minutes past four

○ four-fifteen

○ a quarter to four

5 Which of these clocks shows the time as a quarter to two?

○

○

○

○

Challenge

Which clock shows a half an hour after 6:15?

○

○

○

○

Colorful Clues

You can compare two things that are not alike in order
to give your readers a clearer and more colorful picture.
When you use *like* or *as* to make a comparison, it is called a **simile**.

> *Max is as slow as molasses when he doesn't want to do something.*
> *My sister leaped over the puddles like a frog to avoid getting her shoes wet.*
> *The angry man erupted like a volcano.*

When you make a comparison without *like* or *as*, it is called a **metaphor**.
You compare things directly, saying the subject is something else.

> *The disturbed anthill was a whirlwind of activity.*
> *The oak trees, silent sentries around the cabin, stood guard.*
> *Jenny and I were all ears as we listened to the latest gossip.*

Finish the metaphors and similes.

1. Crowds of commuters piled into the subway cars like _____

   _____ .

2. Chirping crickets on a warm summer night are _____

   _____ .

3. After rolling in the mud, our dog looked like _____ .

4. Happiness is _____ .

5. Just learning to walk, the toddler was as wobbly as _____

   _____ .

6. After scoring the winning point, I felt as _____

   _____ .

7. Having a tooth filled is about as much fun as _____

   _____ .

8. _____ is like _____ .

Working With Area

The **area** of an object is the number of square units needed to cover its surface.
To find the area, multiply the length by the width.

4 x 2 = 8 square units

Write a number sentence to find the area of each shape. Then, on another sheet of paper, write the multiplication and division fact family for each number sentence.

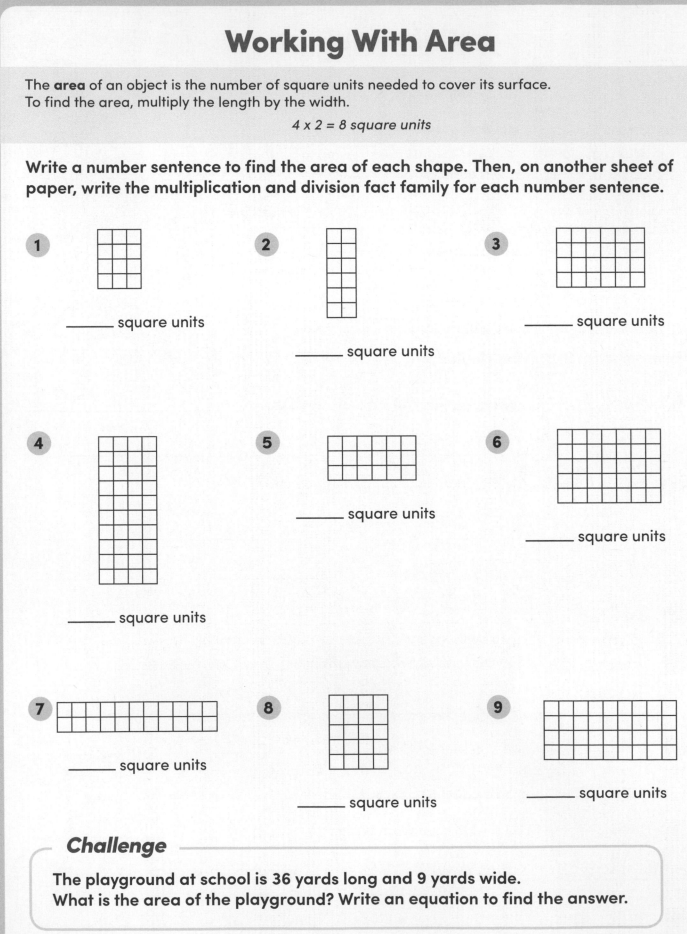

1 _____ square units

2 _____ square units

3 _____ square units

4 _____ square units

5 _____ square units

6 _____ square units

7 _____ square units

8 _____ square units

9 _____ square units

Challenge

The playground at school is 36 yards long and 9 yards wide.
What is the area of the playground? Write an equation to find the answer.

Where's the Action?

A **verb** tells the action in a sentence.

Fill in the bubble beneath the word that is a verb.

1 Did you know that bats are the only mammals that can fly?
   ○   ○   ○   ○

2 Many people fear bats, but bats are really very important to us.
      ○   ○   ○   ○

3 Bats eat half their body weight in bugs every night.
   ○   ○   ○   ○

4 Most bats are harmless to humans and valuable to nature's balance.
        ○   ○   ○   ○

5 Bat mothers generally produce only one baby each year.
   ○   ○   ○   ○

6 Bats usually live in caves or other dark places.
      ○   ○   ○   ○

7 Each year, vandals destroy thousands of bats by blocking cave entrances.
         ○   ○   ○   ○

8 Bats are not really blind, but some people believe they are.
      ○   ○   ○   ○

9 As for the belief that bats carry rabies, this is untrue.
   ○   ○   ○   ○

10 You're more likely to be hit by a falling star than to get rabies from a bat.
           ○   ○   ○   ○

How Many Square Units?

Shade in a shape that matches the given area. The first one is done for you.

1 6 square units

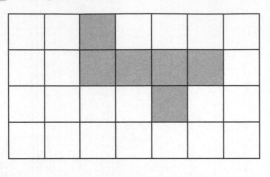

5 8 square units

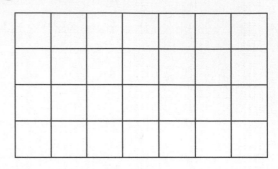

2 10 square units

6 12 square units

3 15 square units

7 21 square units

4 24 square units

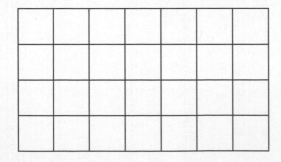

8 25 square units

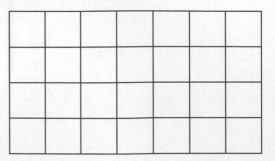

Let's Eat Out!

Two sentences can be combined to make one sentence by using the words *although, after, because, until,* and *while.*

Choose a word from the menu to combine the two sentences into one sentence.

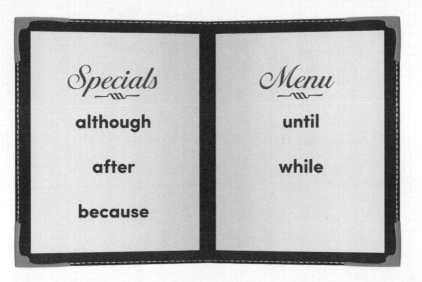

Specials

although

after

because

Menu

until

while

1 We are eating out tonight. Mom worked late.

_____

2 We are going to Joe's Fish Shack. I do not like fish.

_____

3 Dad said I can play outside. It's time to leave.

_____

4 We can play video games. We are waiting for our food.

_____

5 We may stop by Ida's Ice Cream Shop. We leave the restaurant.

_____

_____

Picture Perfect

An **array** shows a multiplication sentence. The first factor tells how many rows there are. The second factor tells how many are in each row. Here is an array for the multiplication sentence *4 x 4 = 16*.

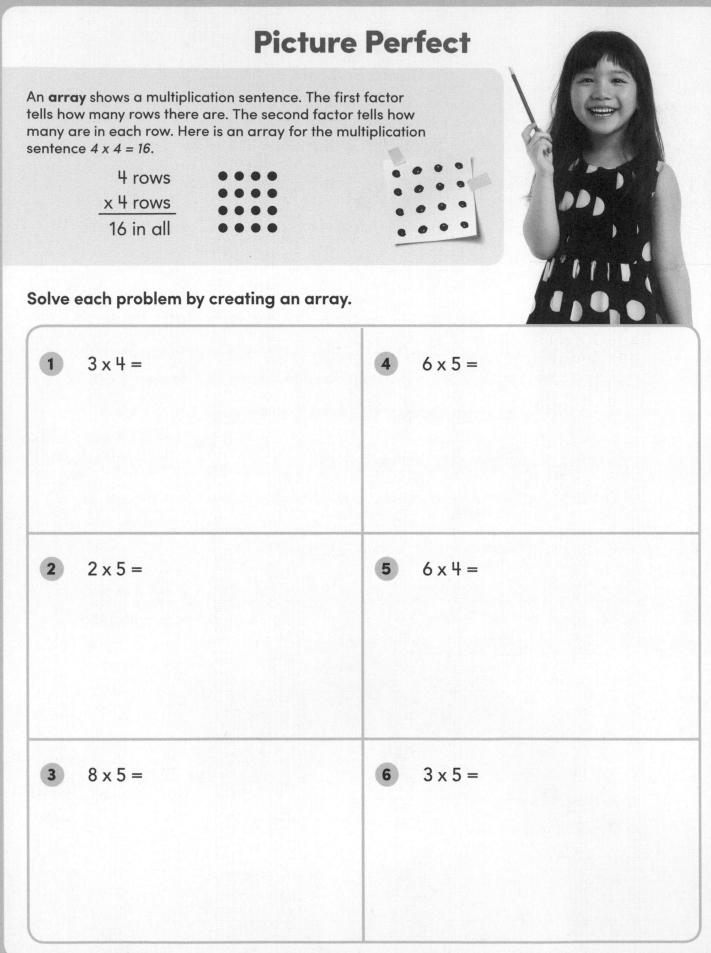

4 rows
x 4 rows
16 in all

Solve each problem by creating an array.

1 3 x 4 =

4 6 x 5 =

2 2 x 5 =

5 6 x 4 =

3 8 x 5 =

6 3 x 5 =

Kadimba's Field
Bantu Folktale

How does Kadimba use his cleverness to avoid work?

1   Clever Kadimba was a lazy hare. It was time to plant crops to feed
2   his family, but he hated work. Tangled bushes throughout his field
3   made the job daunting. Even after clearing the field, Kadimba would
4   still have to dig rows for his crops.

5   Kadimba hatched a plan. He dragged a thick rope across his field.
6   Then he waited by one end for Elephant to appear. Kadimba dared
7   Elephant to a tug-of-war. Elephant roared but agreed. He twisted
8   his trunk around the rope. Kadimba said, "When you feel my pull,
9   then pull back." He raced to the opposite side of the tangled field
10   and rested by the other end of the rope. Elephant waited patiently.

11   Soon Hippo waddled by. Kadimba offered this giant the same
12   challenge. Hippo agreed, letting the hare wrap the rope around his
13   muddy body. Kadimba said, "When you feel my pull, then pull
14   back." Hippo waited good-naturedly.

15   Kadimba then dashed to the middle of the rope and tugged in
16   each direction. Feeling the pull, Elephant and Hippo began tugging.
17   They yanked, grunted, and
18   heaved in astonishment.
19   They pulled back and forth,
20   left and right, struggling
21   until nightfall. By then, the
22   rope had torn out all
23   the tangled bushes; the
24   thrashing had softened the
25   soil. Kadimba's field was
26   ready for planting.

Kadimba's Field (continued)

Answer each question. Give evidence from the folktale.

1 The **daunting** job (line 3) made Kadimba feel _____ .

○ heartbroken   ○ discouraged   ○ sleepy   ○ proud

How did you choose your answer? _____

_____

2 Which type of character is Kadimba? _____ .

○ a brave hero   ○ a sneaky trickster

○ an angry loser   ○ an innocent victim

What in the text helped you answer? _____

_____

_____

_____

3 Why did Hippo and Elephant feel so astonished (line 17–18)._____

_____

_____

4 Why did Kadimba rest for a while (lines 9–11)?_____

_____

5 Explain Kadimba's clever plan. _____

_____

_____

_____

Help Your Child Get Ready: Week 6

Here are some activities that you and your child might enjoy.

Quick Look

Ask your child to look around your kitchen and find 10 or more items that begin with the letter *s*.

Listen Up

Help your child develop good listening and memorization skills. Read the names of the first five presidents of the United States (listed below) two times. Then ask your child to repeat the list back to you in order.

> George Washington, John Adams, Thomas Jefferson, James Madison, and James Monroe

Birthday Futures

Have your child figure out what day of the week his or her birthday will fall on this year, next year, and the year after that. Ask him or her to describe any pattern he or she notices.

Vegetable Know-How

The vegetables we eat come from different parts of plants. Ask your child to keep track of the vegetables you eat for dinner for one week. Then have him or her create a chart to show which part of the plant each vegetable comes from.

These are the skills your child will be working on this week.

Math

- solve word problems using multiplication
- solve word problems using division
- understand multiplication
- multiply by multiples of 10
- round to the nearest 100

Reading

- use visuals
- identify key details

Phonics & Vocabulary

- homonyms

Grammar & Writing

- possessives and plurals
- verb tenses
- build a paragraph: supporting sentences

Incentive Chart: Week 6

Week 6	Day 1	Day 2	Day 3	Day 4	Day 5
Put a sticker to show you completed each day's work.	☆ ☆	☆ ☆	☆ ☆	☆ ☆	☆ ☆

CONGRATULATIONS!

Wow! You did a great job this week!

This certificate is presented to:

_____

_____   _____
Date   Parent/Caregiver's Signature

The Apology of Goldilocks

Goldilocks feels guilty about messing up the home of the three bears. She wants to make it up to them. But she doesn't understand the laws of possessive words. Can you help her?

Wherever you see a blank line, decide whether the word needs an 's, an s', or a plain s. Write your answer on the blank.

Dear Mama Bear, Papa Bear, and Baby Bear,

　　I owe you guy____ an apology. I didn't mean to get my germ____ all over everyone____ porridge and break Baby Bear____ chair. I didn't say to myself, "I think I'll head to the bear____ cottage and mess up their stuff." I had been hiking through the wood____, gathering rock____ for my science project. I had stuffed all the rocks into my jumper____ pocket. When I sat down in Baby Bear____ chair, the rock____ weight caused me to crush the chair!

　　To make it up to you, I would like you to come to my family____ house for dinner. I have a new chair for Baby Bear. (I used all my baby-sitting money to pay for it.) Please let me know if you can come.

Love,

Goldilocks

P.S. I'll be serving some of my parent____ homemade honey.

Grammar Clues

Remember these basic laws of possessives and plurals:

- **Singular possessive ('s):** Use **'s** when you want to show that something belongs to someone or something.

  (Example: *That is **Bozo's** clown wig*.)

- **Plural possessive (s'):** Use **s'** when something belongs to more than one person.

  (Example: *Those are the **clowns'** wigs*.)

- **Plural noun (s):** Use a plain **s** when you simply want to show that there is more than one of something.

  (Example: *There are lots of **clowns** in town. They are all wearing **wigs**.*)

Number Fun With Barky

Write a number sentence for each problem. Solve.

1 Connor's dog, Barky, made 3 holes in the backyard. Connor's dad had to fill each hole with 78 scoops of dirt. How many scoops did his dad need in all?

4 Terri took Barky to the vet for 3 shots. Each shot cost $22.65. How much money did Terri pay the vet?

2 Barky got into Steve's closet. He chewed up 8 pairs of shoes. How many shoes did he chew altogether?

5 Max's job is to keep Barky's water bowl full. If he fills it 3 times a day for 24 days, how many times did he fill the bowl altogether?

3 Adrienne went to the store to buy doggie treats. She bought 6 boxes of doggie treats. Each box has 48 treats. How many treats in all did Adrienne buy?

6 Barky runs around the block 4 times every day. How many times does he run around the block in 5 days?

Two for One

Many words have more than one meaning. These words are called **homonyms**.
Use the other words in the sentence to help determine the meaning of a homonym.

Read each sentence below. Replace the underlined word or words with a homonym from the Word Bank. Use each word in the Word Bank twice.

Word Bank

case	sole	count	band	firm

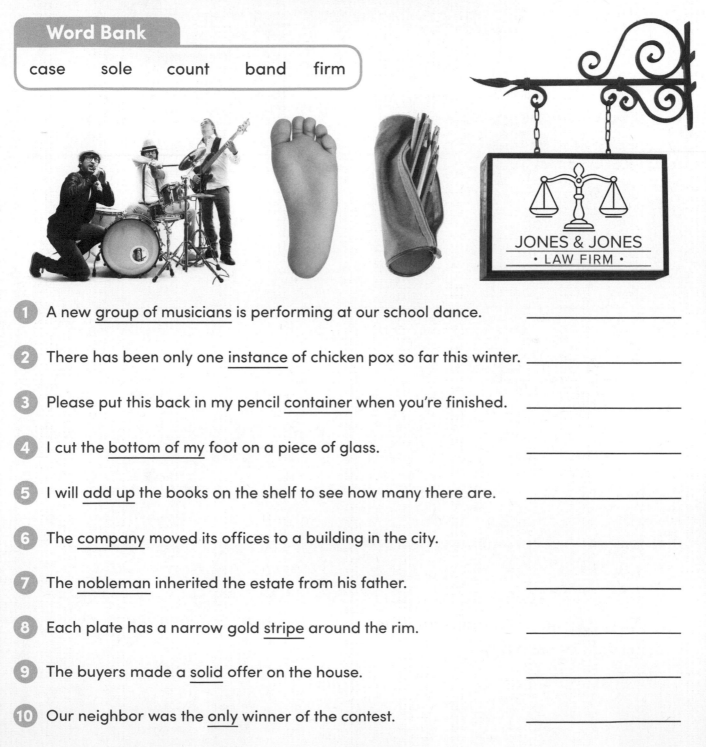

JONES & JONES
· LAW FIRM ·

1 A new group of musicians is performing at our school dance. _____

2 There has been only one instance of chicken pox so far this winter. _____

3 Please put this back in my pencil container when you're finished. _____

4 I cut the bottom of my foot on a piece of glass. _____

5 I will add up the books on the shelf to see how many there are. _____

6 The company moved its offices to a building in the city. _____

7 The nobleman inherited the estate from his father. _____

8 Each plate has a narrow gold stripe around the rim. _____

9 The buyers made a solid offer on the house. _____

10 Our neighbor was the only winner of the contest. _____

Division Treats

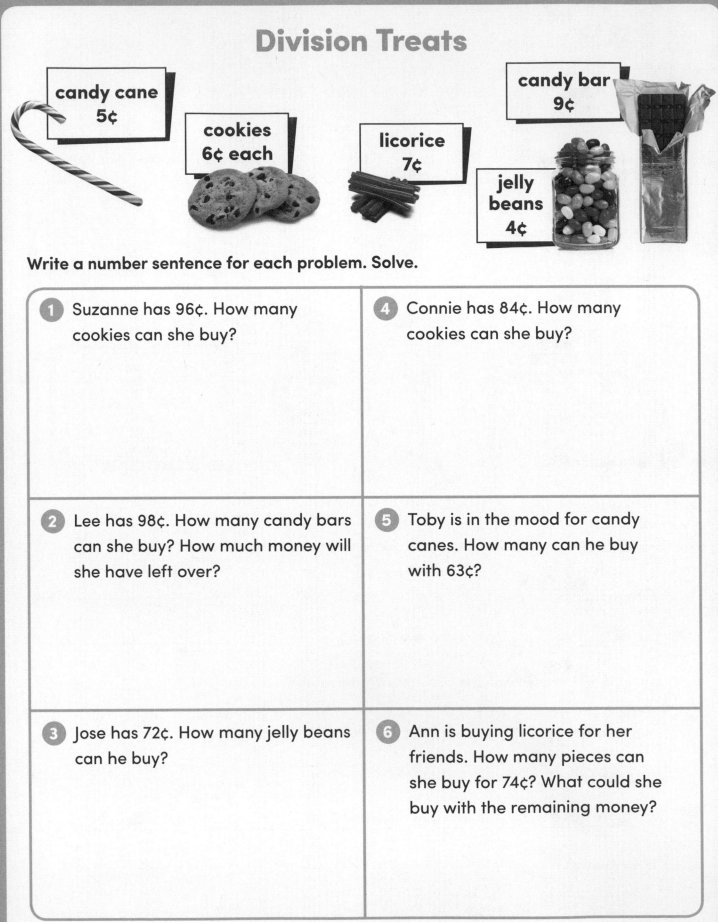

candy cane
5¢

cookies
6¢ each

licorice
7¢

candy bar
9¢

jelly
beans
4¢

Write a number sentence for each problem. Solve.

1 Suzanne has 96¢. How many cookies can she buy?

4 Connie has 84¢. How many cookies can she buy?

2 Lee has 98¢. How many candy bars can she buy? How much money will she have left over?

5 Toby is in the mood for candy canes. How many can he buy with 63¢?

3 Jose has 72¢. How many jelly beans can he buy?

6 Ann is buying licorice for her friends. How many pieces can she buy for 74¢? What could she buy with the remaining money?

Present- and Past-Tense Verbs

Present-tense verbs show action that is happening now.
They agree in number with who or what is doing the action.
Past-tense verbs show action that took place in the past. Most past-tense verbs end in *-ed*.

A. Read each sentence. If the underlined verb is in the present tense, write *present* on the line. If it is in the past tense, write *past*.

1 We <u>worked</u> together on a jigsaw puzzle. _____

2 Mom <u>helped</u> us. _____

3 She <u>enjoys</u> puzzles, too. _____

4 Tom <u>picked</u> out the border pieces. _____

5 He <u>dropped</u> a puzzle piece on the floor. _____

6 I <u>looked</u> for the flower pieces. _____

7 Dad <u>likes</u> crossword puzzles better. _____

8 My little sister <u>watches</u> us. _____

9 Mom <u>hurries</u> us before dinner. _____

10 We <u>rushed</u> to finish quickly. _____

B. Underline the verb in each sentence. Then rewrite the sentence. Change the present-tense verb to the past. Change the past-tense verb to the present.

1 The man crosses the river.

_____

2 He rowed his boat.

_____

Multiply the Groups

Write the number of groups and the number of objects in each group. Then write a complete multiplication fact that relates to each picture. The first one is done for you.

1

3 groups of 8

_3 × 8 = 24_

4

2

5

3

6

That Drives Me Crazy!

The sentences that follow the topic sentence tell more about the topic. They are called **supporting sentences**.

Read the paragraph below. Cross out the three sentences that do not support the topic.

My Pet Peeves

I am a pretty agreeable person, but there are a few things around my house that drive me crazy. One such thing is when my younger brothers go into my bedroom and destroy my building creations. My three-year-old brothers both have brown hair. I also get upset when my sister sings at the dinner table. Her favorite sport is gymnastics. My greatest pet peeve is when my older brother taps his pencil on the kitchen table while I am studying spelling words. I wish I had a fish tank in my room. My brothers and sister are really great, but there are moments when they make me crazy!

Rewrite the paragraph above skipping the sentences that you crossed out. The new paragraph should have one topic sentence followed by the supporting sentences.

_____

_____

_____

_____

_____

_____

_____

Find the Product

Write the product of each statement.

x	1	2	3	4	5	6	7	8	9	10
1	1	2	3	4	5	6	7	8	9	10
2	2	4	6	8	10	12	14	16	18	20
3	3	6	9	12	15	18	21	24	27	30
4	4	8	12	16	20	24	28	32	36	40
5	5	10	15	20	25	30	35	40	45	50
6	6	12	18	24	30	36	42	48	54	60
7	7	14	21	28	35	42	49	56	63	70
8	8	16	24	32	40	48	56	64	72	80
9	9	18	27	36	45	54	63	72	81	90
10	10	20	30	40	50	60	70	80	90	100

1 $7 \times 30 =$ _____

2 $40 \times 7 =$ _____

3 $50 \times 50 =$ _____

4 $9 \times 500 =$ _____

5 $20 \times 600 =$ _____

6 $6 \times 20 =$ _____

7 $60 \times 8 =$ _____

8 $20 \times 90 =$ _____

9 $300 \times 30 =$ _____

10 $9,000 \times 7 =$ _____

11 $50 \times 9 =$ _____

12 $80 \times 3 =$ _____

13 $50 \times 90 =$ _____

14 $70 \times 100 =$ _____

15 $400 \times 20 =$ _____

Honoring King's Dreams

Martin Luther King, Jr. was a great American leader. The national holiday that honors him is on the third Monday in January. King's birthday is January 15.

During the 1950s and 1960s, King worked to end unfair laws. He led peaceful protests and made speeches. In 1963, King gave one of his most important speeches. More than 250,000 people gathered in Washington, D.C. to listen to him. In his speech, King said he dreamed people would be judged not by the color of their skin but by their actions.

King was killed in 1968. In 2011, a memorial opened in Washington, D.C. to honor him. It features a 30-foot statue of King. Americans can visit the memorial to remember King and his message of peace and equality.

Timeline: Martin Luther King, Jr.

1929 King is born in Atlanta, Georgia

1954 King becomes the pastor of a church in Montgomery, Alabama

1963 King gives his "I Have a Dream" speech

1965 King leads a march from Selma, Alabama to Montgomery, Alabama, to demand equal voting rights for African Americans

1968 King is killed in Memphis, Tennessee

1930   1940   1950   1960   1970

1 What did King accomplish in 1954? _____

_____

2 What was the purpose of the march that King led in Alabama in 1965?

_____

3 In his 1963 speech, how did Martin Luther King, Jr. say that people should be judged?

○ by the color of their skin   ○ by their actions

○ by the speeches they give   ○ by how famous they are

4 According to the article, what did King try to end?

○ wars   ○ crime   ○ protests   ○ unfair laws

Rounding to Hundreds

Round each value to the nearest hundred.
Draw a line to match each answer on the left with one on the right.

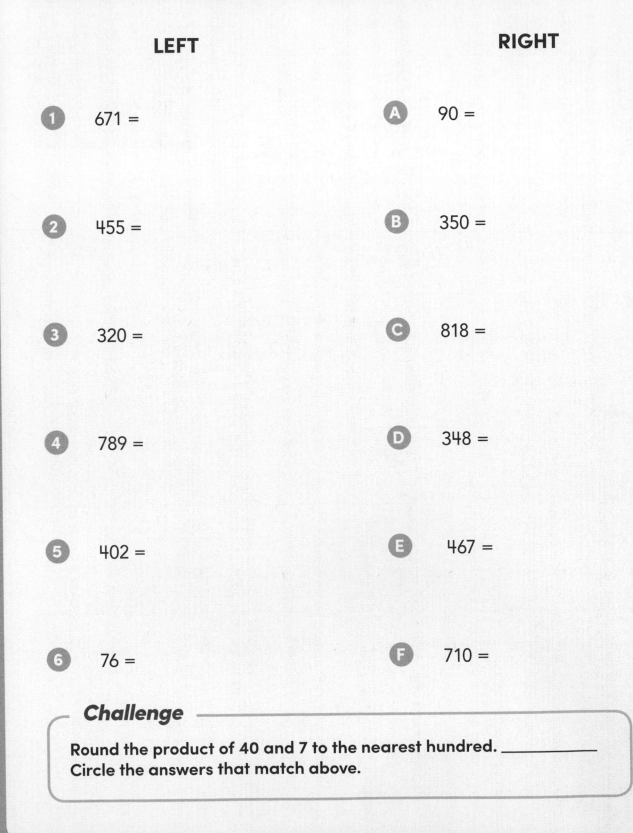

LEFT

RIGHT

1 671 =

A 90 =

2 455 =

B 350 =

3 320 =

C 818 =

4 789 =

D 348 =

5 402 =

E 467 =

6 76 =

F 710 =

Challenge

Round the product of 40 and 7 to the nearest hundred. _____
Circle the answers that match above.

Help Your Child Get Ready: Week 7

Here are some activities that you and your child might enjoy.

Mum's the Word

This is a fun dinnertime family game. Agree on a small word that is used frequently in conversation, such as *the* or *and*. This word becomes "mum." No one can say it! Anyone who does, drops out. The last person left is the winner.

Palindrome Collection

Palindromes are words that are spelled the same backward and forward. Start a palindrome collection with your child. Here are some to get you going: *bob, civic, eye, Anna,* and *refer.*

One-Minute Categories

Ask your child to name as many examples as possible of a particular category in one minute. For example, for animals, he or she might name *dog, cat, zebra, horse,* and so on. Make the categories more challenging as his or her skill increases.

What's the Math Question?

Ask your child to make up a question or problem to go with an answer. For example, if you say the answer is "48," he or she could say the question is "What is 12 x 4?" or "What is 54 – 6?"

These are the skills your child will be working on this week.

Math

- recognize and generate equivalent fractions
- make a pictograph
- solve word problems using division
- calculate area

Reading

- identify setting
- analyze characters
- recognize point of view

Phonics & Vocabulary

- idioms
- suffixes: *–ness, –ful, – ly, –ment, –er*

Grammar & Writing

- irregular verbs
- expand sentences

Incentive Chart: Week 7

Week 7	Day 1	Day 2	Day 3	Day 4	Day 5
Put a sticker to show you completed each day's work.	☆ ☆	☆ ☆	☆ ☆	☆ ☆	☆ ☆

CONGRATULATIONS!

Wow! You did a great job this week!

This certificate is presented to:

_____

_____   _____
Date   Parent/Caregiver's Signature

Piece of Cake!

Piece of cake is an example of a common **idiom**, or expression. It means "an easy task." It is difficult to understand the meaning of the idiom by using the ordinary meaning of the words.

What does the idiom in each sentence mean? Fill in the bubble next to the meaning that makes the most sense.

1 Jason was so tired that he **hit the hay** right after dinner.

- ○ went to bed
- ○ went back to work
- ○ cut the grass

2 Do not waste your money on this video because it is **for the birds**.

- ○ worthless
- ○ fantastic
- ○ expensive

3 Jasmine was **down in the dumps** after losing the game.

- ○ smelly
- ○ excited
- ○ sad

4 "Classical music is definitely **not my cup of tea**," said Trey's grandmother.

- ○ not cheap
- ○ not to my liking
- ○ not hot enough

5 Ben and Lisa do not **see eye to eye** about which movie to watch.

- ○ disagree
- ○ agree
- ○ argue

6 "I don't recall his name," said Kim, "but his face **rings a bell**."

- ○ is unfamiliar
- ○ stirs a memory
- ○ appears

7 Carlos has been **on cloud nine** since winning the contest.

- ○ very unhappy
- ○ unfriendly
- ○ joyous

8 The two old men were sitting on the park bench **chewing the fat**.

- ○ feeding the squirrels
- ○ having a friendly chat
- ○ eating lunch

It's All the Same!

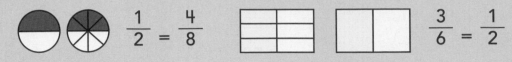

Equivalent fractions have the same amount.

$$\frac{1}{2} = \frac{4}{8} \qquad \frac{3}{6} = \frac{1}{2}$$

Write each missing numerator to show equivalent fractions.

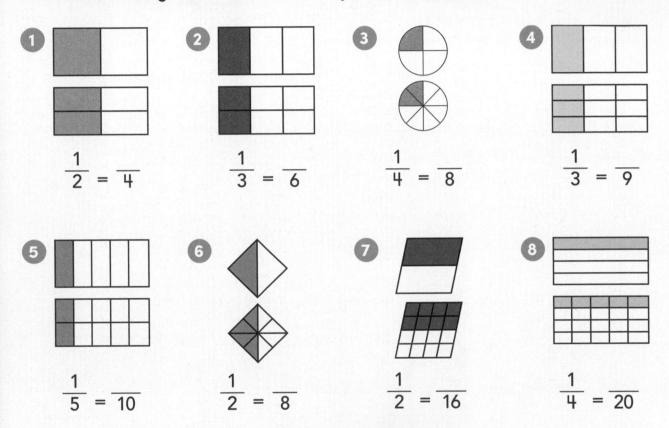

1 $\dfrac{1}{2} = \dfrac{}{4}$

2 $\dfrac{1}{3} = \dfrac{}{6}$

3 $\dfrac{1}{4} = \dfrac{}{8}$

4 $\dfrac{1}{3} = \dfrac{}{9}$

5 $\dfrac{1}{5} = \dfrac{}{10}$

6 $\dfrac{1}{2} = \dfrac{}{8}$

7 $\dfrac{1}{2} = \dfrac{}{16}$

8 $\dfrac{1}{4} = \dfrac{}{20}$

Write the number sentence that shows each set of equivalent fractions.

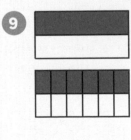
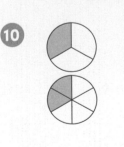
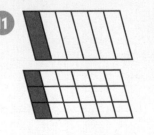
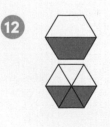

9 $\dfrac{}{} = \dfrac{}{}$

10 $\dfrac{}{} = \dfrac{}{}$

11 $\dfrac{}{} = \dfrac{}{}$

12 $\dfrac{}{} = \dfrac{}{}$

Irregular Verbs

Irregular verbs do not form the past tense by adding -ed. They change their form.

A. In each sentence, underline the past tense of the verb in parentheses. Then, write the past-tense verb on the line.

1 Jessie told Jamal to be ready early. (tell) _____

2 He was nervous about his science fair project. (is) _____

3 Jamal's friends came to the table. (come) _____

4 They saw the volcano there. (see) _____

5 Jamal knew his speech by heart. (know) _____

6 The sign on the exhibit fell over. (fall) _____

7 The teacher lit the match for Jamal. (light) _____

8 Jamal threw his hands into the air. (throw) _____

B. Use a word from the Word Bank to complete each sentence.

1 Jamal _____ all about volcanoes.

2 He once _____ a real volcano.

3 It _____ ashes and fire into the air.

4 The ashes _____ all over the ground.

Word Bank	
fell	threw
saw	knew

C. Complete each sentence. Use the past forms of *know* in one and the past form of *tell* in the other two.

1 When I was five, I _____

2 My brother _____

3 Last week, _____

85

Creature Count

A pictograph uses symbols to represent data. Use the chart on the right and the information in the problems below to make a pictograph.

Number of Select Animals at London Zoo, January 2012	
Blue Spiny Lizard	25
Moon Jellyfish	90
Short-Tailed Bat	200
Naked Mole Rat	35
Rasbora (fish)	65

1 Label the rows in the vertical axis of your graph with the name of each animal. What should you label the horizontal axis?

_____

2 Decide on an icon for your pictograph. Each icon will represent the same number of animals. The icon should be easy to draw, and you should also be able to draw half of one. Draw your icon in the box.

3 Decide how many animals will be represented by each icon. Which number will allow you to best represent your data?

○ 5   ○ 10   ○ 100

4 Draw your graph below. Make sure it has a title, labels, and icons based on the data in the chart. Add a key that explains how many animals each icon represents.

Title: _____

Vertical axis

Horizontal axis title: _____

Graph Key:

Suffixes

A **suffix** is a word part that is added to the end of a word.
A suffix changes the meaning of a word.

-ness and *-ment* mean "a state of being"	*-ly* means "in that way"
-ful means "full of"	*-er* means "a person who acts as"

A. Underline the suffix in each word below.
Write the number of the word next to its definition on the right.

1 **darkness**

2 **government**

3 **graceful**

4 **rapidly**

5 **rancher**

_____ to do something in a quick way

_____ a person who works on a ranch

_____ a group that governs a city, state or nation

_____ moving in a smooth way, full of grace

_____ the state of being dark

B. Add a suffix to each word to form a new word.
Use the meaning in parentheses to help you.

1 eager _____
(state of being)

2 catch _____
(one who does something)

3 plenti _____
(full of)

4 paint _____
(one who does something)

5 distant _____
(in that way)

6 amaze _____
(state of being)

C. Read the words. Write a word that means almost the same thing.

1 fast, speedily, quickly _____

2 surprise, astonishment, shock _____

3 much, lots, boundless _____

4 beautiful, elegant, charming _____

Figure It Out

The **quotient** tells how many equal groups you can make.
The **remainder** tells how many are left over.

Divide. Answer each question.

1 A clothing store clerk has 14 sweaters. He wants to put them in equal stacks on 3 shelves. How many sweaters will be in each stack?

2 Mary needs to bake 71 cookies. Each cookie sheet holds 8 cookies. How many cookies are on the unfilled cookie sheet?

3 Luis is putting 74 cans into cartons. Each carton holds 8 cans. How many cans will be in the unfilled carton?

4 Rosa has 57¢. She wants to buy lollipops that cost 9¢ each. How many lollipops can she buy?

5 There are 17 cars waiting to be parked. There are an equal number of parking spots on 3 different levels. How many cars will not find a parking spot?

6 Don bought 85 crates of flowers. He separated them into groups of 9. How many equal groups did he have?

Where Are We Going?

A sentence includes a **subject** and a **verb**.
A sentence is more interesting when it also includes
a part that tells *where, when,* or *why*.

Add more information to each sentence by telling
where, when, or *why*. **Write the complete new sentence.**

1 Mom is taking us shopping.

When?

_____
_____

2 The stores are closing.

When?

_____
_____

3 We need to find a gift for dad.

Why?

_____
_____

4 I will buy new jeans.

Where?

_____
_____

5 We may eat lunch.

Where?

_____
_____

Calculating Area

Find the area of each shape in square units. Each small square has an area of 1 square unit. If you need to, fill in the missing lines.

Follow the directions to complete each model.

1
Area = _____ square units

6
Area = _____ square units

2
Area = _____ square units

7
Area = _____ square units

3
Area = _____ square units

8
Area = _____ square units

4
Area = _____ square units

9
Area = _____ square units

5
Area = _____ square units

10
Area = _____ square units

11 Draw a rectangle that has a length of 7 units and an area of 14 square units.

12 Draw a square that has an area of 25 square units.

13 Draw a rectangle with a length of 8 units and a width of 6 units.

14 Draw a rectangle with a width of 5 units and an area of 35 square units.

The area of an object is the number of square units needed to cover its surface. Multiply the length by the width to find the area.

Follow Me

What makes this story an adventure?

1 "When this volcano blew about a thousand years ago,
2 it sent the local inhabitants scurrying to safety," Mimi
3 reported as we neared our destination.
4 We drove through a moonlike landscape, where plants
5 and trees struggled to grow. Then I saw Sunset Crater. It
6 was a huge black cone with tinges of orange and yellow.
7 It was magnificent! We parked the car and began to walk
8 the winding trail along its base. "I've got the flashlights,"
9 Mimi said.
10 Flashlights? I wondered. I soon found out the
11 reason for them when she
12 stopped and pointed to a
13 narrow, dark opening. "Follow
14 me," she called. "We're about
15 to enter a tunnel made by
16 lava. Zip up your sweatshirt."
17 We scrambled down into
18 darkness. It got cold very
19 quickly as we descended; it
20 got scary, too. We clambered

21 over sharp and slippery rocks and had to duck under
22 hanging rocks that looked like icicles. The ceiling was so
23 low in parts that we had to crawl. Soon the walls began to
24 close in on us. At that point we stopped, took in the eerie
25 silence, and then made our way out.
26 "Amazing lava tube, right?" Mimi asked, once we were
27 safely above ground.
28 "Awesome!" I answered, relieved to see blue sky.

Follow Me (continued)

Answer each question. Give evidence from the adventure.

1 If you **descended** (line 19), you

○ climbed up   ○ went down   ○ wondered   ○ explored

How did you pick your answer? _____

_____

2 Which sentence best describes a lava tube (line 26)?

○ It is a tunnel made by lava.   ○ It is a kind of volcano.

○ It is a moonlike landscape.   ○ It is a winding trail.

What in the text helped you answer? _____

_____

3 Why did Mimi bring along flashlights?

_____

_____

_____

4 What would be scary about going into a lava tube for the first time? Explain.

_____

_____

5 Explain what "the walls began to close in on us" (lines 23 and 24) means?

_____

_____

_____

Help Your Child Get Ready: Week 8

Here are some activities that you and your child might enjoy.

Word Chain

Develop your child's listening skills by playing "Word Chain." In this game, someone says a word, and the next person must say a word that begins with the last letter of the previous player's word.

Movie Review

Ask your child to write a movie review. Be sure he or she writes the review immediately after the movie—just like real critics do. Encourage him or her to include lots of descriptive words in the review.

Poems to Remember

Encourage your child to memorize a short poem. Doing so will require him or her to read a poem over and over—a great way to build reading fluency. You might suggest a poem by Bruce Lansky, Kenn Nesbitt, Jack Prelutsky, or Shel Silverstein. Give your child plenty of time to learn the poem and then give him or her a chance to recite it to the rest of the family.

Bug Safari

Have your child go on a bug safari! Mark off a small section of your backyard or a park. Then start hunting. Have him or her keep a list of the different kinds of bugs he or she sees. You might want to have a field guide handy so bug identification is easy.

These are the skills your child will be working on this week.

Math
- division with remainders
- use line plots
- compare fractions
- recognize and use units of measure
- commutative properties of multiplication

Reading
- compare and contrast

Phonics & Vocabulary
- homographs

Grammar & Writing
- adverbs
- adjectives
- build a paragraph: supporting sentences

Incentive Chart: Week 8

Week 8	Day 1	Day 2	Day 3	Day 4	Day 5
Put a sticker to show you completed each day's work.	☆ ☆	☆ ☆	☆ ☆	☆ ☆	☆ ☆

CONGRATULATIONS!

Wow! You did a great job this week!

This certificate is presented to:

_____

_____   _____
Date   Parent/Caregiver's Signature

Describe the Action

Adverbs can tell when, where, how, or how much.

Most deserts in the United States are very hot and dry. Plants and animals have adapted to live in deserts. For example, many plants have far-reaching roots to search for water. Some cacti swell up to to store water. Animals have also developed varied ways of dealing with the heat and lack of water.

Use what you know to draw conclusions about desert plants and animals. Answer the questions below using one or more of the adverbs from the Word Bank. Complete the sentences.

Word Bank

always	eagerly	loudly	rarely
slowly	occasionally	usually	very

1 When does it rain in the desert?

It _____ rains in the desert.

2 How do most animals move in the heat?

Most animals move _____ .

3 How does a cactus grow?

A cactus grows _____ .

4 How do thirsty creatures drink?

Thirsty creatures drink

_____ .

5 How often should you drink water when you are in the desert?

When I am in the desert, I should

_____

_____ .

Over the Hurdles

Sometimes when you try to divide a number into equal groups, part of the number is left over. This is called the **remainder**. Use these steps to find the remainder.

1. $5\overline{)16}$

Think: 5 x ____ is the closest to 16?

2. $\begin{array}{r} 3 \\ 5\overline{)16} \\ -15 \\ \hline 1 \end{array}$

3. $\begin{array}{r} 3\ R\ 1 \\ 5\overline{)16} \\ -15 \\ \hline 1 \end{array}$

There are 5 groups of 3 with 1 left over.

Divide.

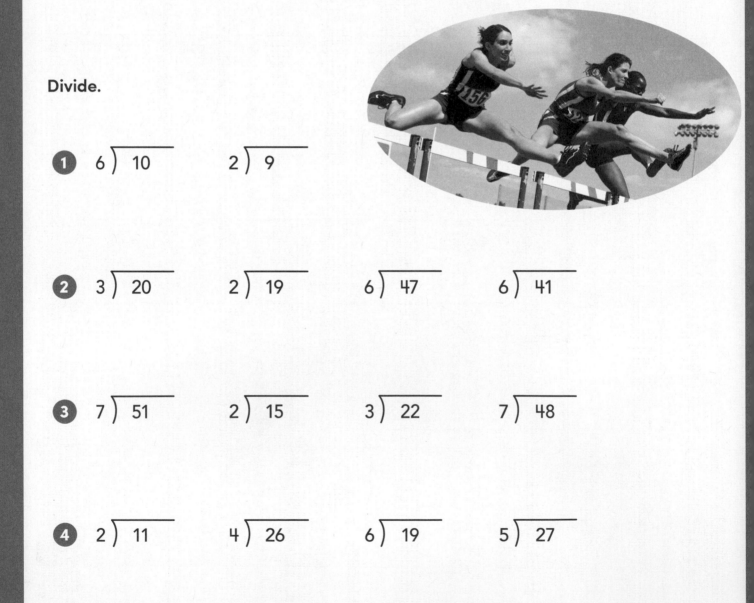

1 $6\overline{)10}$ $2\overline{)9}$

2 $3\overline{)20}$ $2\overline{)19}$ $6\overline{)47}$ $6\overline{)41}$

3 $7\overline{)51}$ $2\overline{)15}$ $3\overline{)22}$ $7\overline{)48}$

4 $2\overline{)11}$ $4\overline{)26}$ $6\overline{)19}$ $5\overline{)27}$

Which One Do You Mean?

Say both pronunciations for each homograph. Then write the letter for the correct pronunciation for the homographs in the sentences. Use a dictionary if you are not sure of the meaning of a word.

Homographs are words that have the same spellings but different meanings and pronunciations.

For example, when you refer to a female hog, *sow* rhymes with *cow*. When you scatter seeds, *sow* rhymes with *no*.

---

refuse	**a. (ref**-yoos)	minute	**a. (min**-it)	close	**a. (klohz)**
	b. (ri-**fyooz**)		**b.** (mye-**noot**)		**b. (klohss)**
wound	**a. (wound)**	object	**a. (ob**-jikt)	bow	**a. (bou)**
	b. (woond)		**b.** (uhb-**jekt**)		**b. (boh)**

---

1 Give me a **minute** _____ to adjust the microscope,

so you can clearly see the **minute** _____ germs.

2 The doctor cleaned the **wound** _____ on my arm and then **wound**

_____ a bandage around it.

3 I **refuse** _____ to carry the **refuse** _____ to the dumpster

unless it is all in a sealed plastic bag.

4 Please **close** _____ the window that is **close** _____ to my desk.

5 The **bow** _____ in my hair fell out as I gave a **bow** _____ after my recital.

6 Would you **object** _____ if I put this **object** _____ on your desk?

Plot It!

Create a line plot based on the given numbers.

1 1, 4, 5, 4, 7, 5, 4, 3, 5

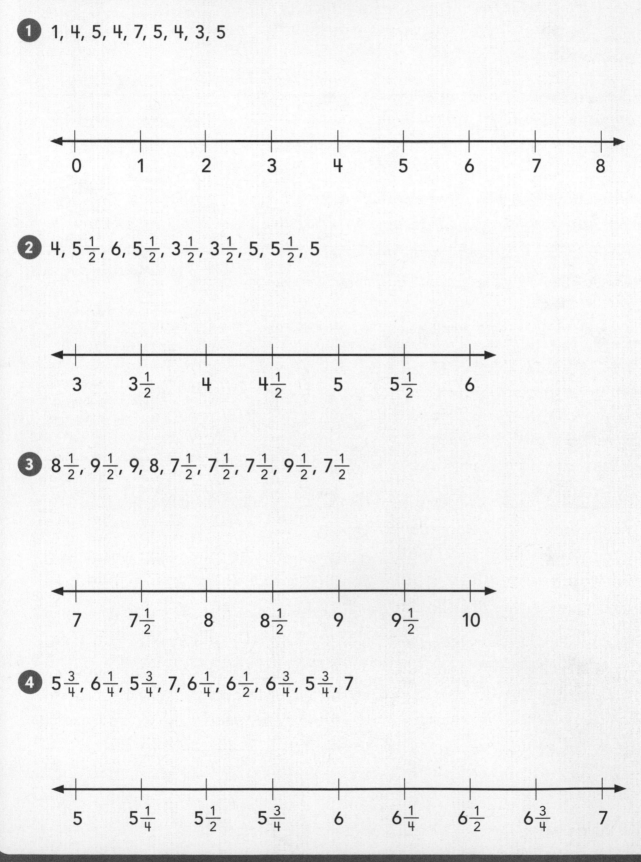

2 4, $5\frac{1}{2}$, 6, $5\frac{1}{2}$, $3\frac{1}{2}$, $3\frac{1}{2}$, 5, $5\frac{1}{2}$, 5

3 $8\frac{1}{2}$, $9\frac{1}{2}$, 9, 8, $7\frac{1}{2}$, $7\frac{1}{2}$, $7\frac{1}{2}$, $9\frac{1}{2}$, $7\frac{1}{2}$

4 $5\frac{3}{4}$, $6\frac{1}{4}$, $5\frac{3}{4}$, 7, $6\frac{1}{4}$, $6\frac{1}{2}$, $6\frac{3}{4}$, $5\frac{3}{4}$, 7

The Case of the Unexpected Delay

Will the Gingerbread Man's delicious new house ever be completed? Not if the hungry workers can help it!

Circle all the adjectives and underline all the adverbs in the letter below.

Dear Mr. Gingerbread Man,

We have some bad news. The big additions you asked us to build on your gingerbread house haven't been going as originally planned. Something strange is happening. Please let me humbly explain.

You must know that coconut lollipops, sticky toffee bars, and giant candy canes are not normal materials for building a new bedroom. But when I asked my loyal employees, they said that they would joyfully welcome the unusual challenge. Big Tony was especially excited. He even started anxiously licking his lips.

Grammar Clues

- An **adjective** describes a noun or a pronoun. It might tell what kind, which one, or how many.

  (Example: *My two best friends gave me the most wonderful surprise ever!*)

- An **adverb** describes a verb, an adjective, or another adverb. Many adverbs end in *-ly*.

  (Example: *I quickly finished my homework so I could watch TV.*)

On the first day of work, I noticed that we were using up purple gumdrops faster than I'd expected. And the order I had placed for giant jawbreakers was short by nearly a hundred. Then the huge crate of red licorice we were using for the inside walls disappeared!

Suddenly my favorite workers are regularly calling in sick. Heavy Hank told me he had seventeen cavities. He's going to be out for a week getting them professionally drilled. Chubby Chuck has gotten so chubby that he fell through the graham-cracker roof. I don't know what's happening to them. Maybe they need more physical exercise.

Please, just give us more time. We'll quickly do a wonderful job.

Sincerely,

Do-It-All Builders, Inc.

Comparing Fractions

Each pair of fractions has the same denominator.
Compare each pair of fractions. Use the symbols <, >, or =.

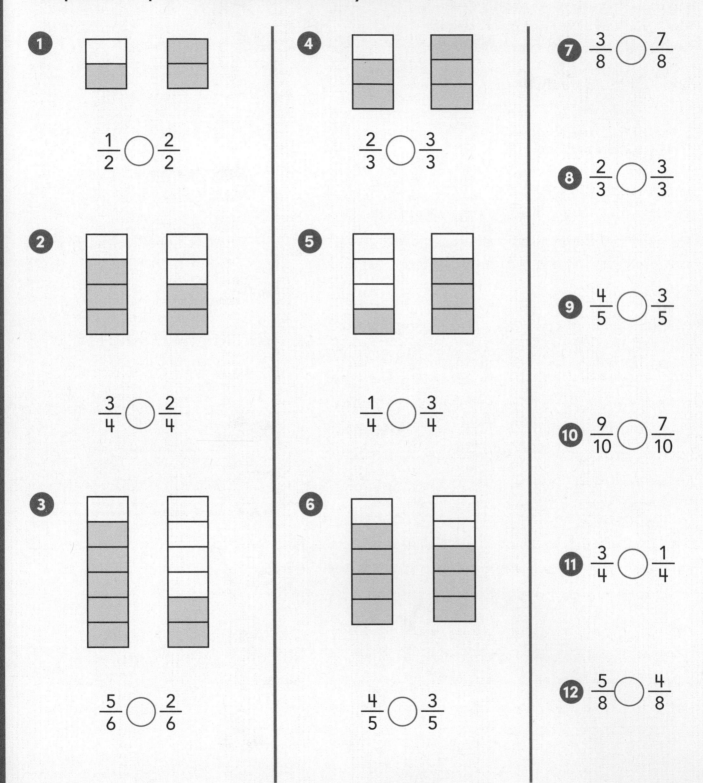

1. $\dfrac{1}{2} \bigcirc \dfrac{2}{2}$

2. $\dfrac{3}{4} \bigcirc \dfrac{2}{4}$

3. $\dfrac{5}{6} \bigcirc \dfrac{2}{6}$

4. $\dfrac{2}{3} \bigcirc \dfrac{3}{3}$

5. $\dfrac{1}{4} \bigcirc \dfrac{3}{4}$

6. $\dfrac{4}{5} \bigcirc \dfrac{3}{5}$

7. $\dfrac{3}{8} \bigcirc \dfrac{7}{8}$

8. $\dfrac{2}{3} \bigcirc \dfrac{3}{3}$

9. $\dfrac{4}{5} \bigcirc \dfrac{3}{5}$

10. $\dfrac{9}{10} \bigcirc \dfrac{7}{10}$

11. $\dfrac{3}{4} \bigcirc \dfrac{1}{4}$

12. $\dfrac{5}{8} \bigcirc \dfrac{4}{8}$

A Great Trick

The sentences that follow the topic sentence tell more about the topic. They are called **supporting sentences**. Supporting sentences should be in an order that makes sense.

Read the topic sentence, then number the supporting ideas from 1 (first) to 4 (last).

Last week I played a great trick on my mom.

_____ won a huge rubber snake

_____ went to a carnival

_____ called my mom outside

_____ put the snake in my mom's flower garden.

Now use the topic sentence and ideas in the correct order to write a paragraph telling the story. Be sure to use complete sentences.

_____

_____

_____

_____

_____

_____

_____

_____

Units of Measure

The side lengths of each rectangle below are labeled.
Find the area of each rectangle. Make sure to label the units correctly.

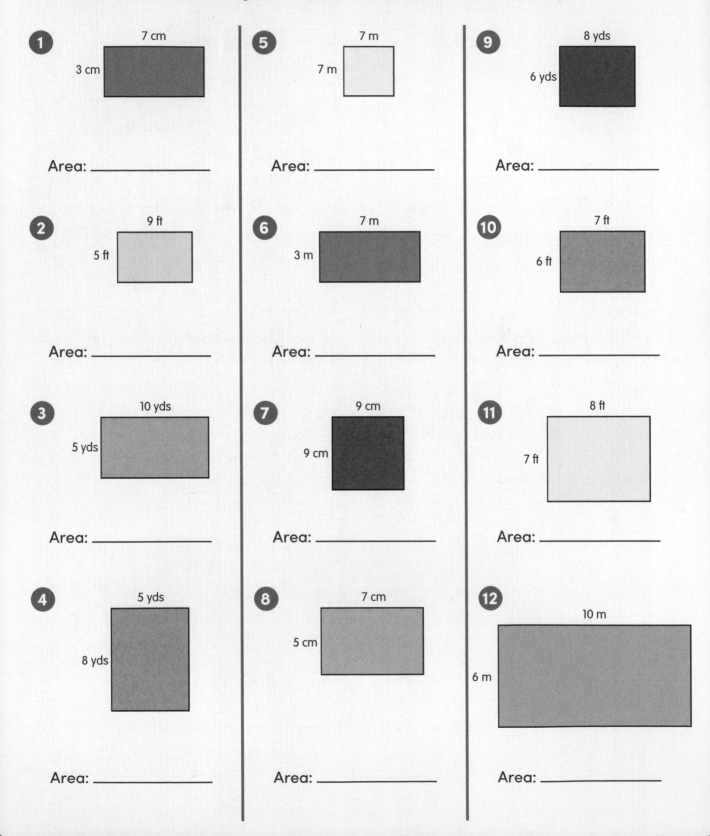

1 7 cm / 3 cm

Area: _____

2 9 ft / 5 ft

Area: _____

3 10 yds / 5 yds

Area: _____

4 5 yds / 8 yds

Area: _____

5 7 m / 7 m

Area: _____

6 7 m / 3 m

Area: _____

7 9 cm / 9 cm

Area: _____

8 7 cm / 5 cm

Area: _____

9 8 yds / 6 yds

Area: _____

10 7 ft / 6 ft

Area: _____

11 8 ft / 7 ft

Area: _____

12 10 m / 6 m

Area: _____

Animal Invaders

Read the articles below. Then answer the questions.

Turkey Trouble

Turkeys are popular animals around Thanksgiving. But some people in Nevada are pretty tired of them. The big birds are taking over a treasured place— Great Basin National Park.

Wild turkeys aren't native to Nevada. Ten years ago, people brought some to the area to hunt them. A few turkeys got inside the park. Their numbers began growing. Now, nearly a thousand turkeys live there.

The birds are gobbling up everything from seeds to mice. Rangers worry that this could leave less food for other animals. To stop the turkeys, they may have to trap the birds and move them to a new place.

Sniffing for Slime

Giant African snails are oozing around in Miami, Florida. The creatures are unwelcome visitors. The snails gobble up crops that people depend on for food.

African snails are an invasive species. Invasive species are plants or animals that live where they don't belong and harm native wildlife and plants. Experts say that the snails were illegally brought to the U.S. from Africa. Some escaped and quickly multiplied.

To help get rid of the snails, officials in Miami have trained dogs to locate them. The snails leave behind a stinky trail of slime that some dogs can sniff out. The furry detectives are on the hunt for thousands of snails loose in the city.

1 What main idea do the articles "Turkey Trouble" and "Sniffing for Slime" share? Cite evidence from each article that supports the main idea.

The main idea is _____

In "Turkey Trouble," we learn that _____

_____

In "Sniffing for Slime," we find out that_____

_____

2 How are officials in Nevada and Florida dealing with the problems?

_____

_____

Multiplication Triangles

Write two facts that illustrate the commutative property of multiplication.
The first one is done for you.

1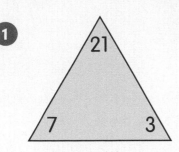

$7 \times 3 = 21$

$3 \times 7 = 21$

2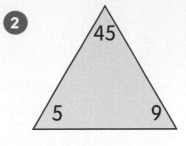

3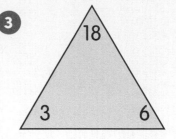

4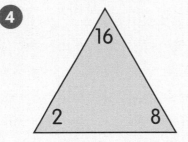

5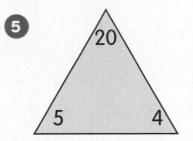

6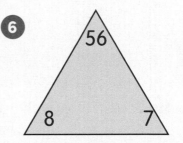

7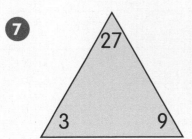

8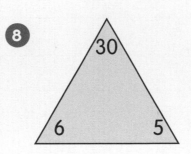

9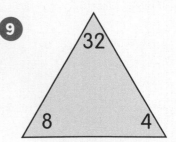

Help Your Child Get Ready: Week 9

Here are some activities that you and your child might enjoy.

Word Box

Create a word box by labeling a small box. Invite family members to put interesting words written on slips of paper into the word box. Once a week, take the slips out and talk about the words with your child.

Family Quiz Show

Have your child host your own family quiz show. He or she will need to spend some time writing up questions. The quiz show can include 40 questions that are sorted into categories. Decide on a prize for the winner before you start.

Shopping List Maker

Invite your child to become your official shopping-list maker. Dictate to him or her all the items you'll need to purchase on your next trip to the grocery store. This is a great way to build spelling skills.

Newspaper Read Aloud

Choose an article from your newspaper that might be of interest to your child. Read it aloud to him or her and then discuss it.

These are the skills your child will be working on this week.

Math

- understand perimeter and area

- fractions: parts of a whole

- associative properties of multiplication

- identify fractions on a number line

- multiplication and division fact families

Reading

- sequence

- compare and contrast

Grammar & Writing

- parts of speech

- subject and object pronouns

- combine sentences

Incentive Chart: Week 9

Week 9	Day 1	Day 2	Day 3	Day 4	Day 5
Put a sticker to show you completed each day's work.	☆ ☆	☆ ☆	☆ ☆	☆ ☆	☆ ☆

CONGRATULATIONS!

Wow! You did a great job this week!

This certificate is presented to:

_____

_____   _____
Date   Parent/Caregiver's Signature

My Summer Vacation

Don't read the story yet! Write a word for the parts of speech listed under the blanks on the left. Then write the words in the story and read the story aloud.

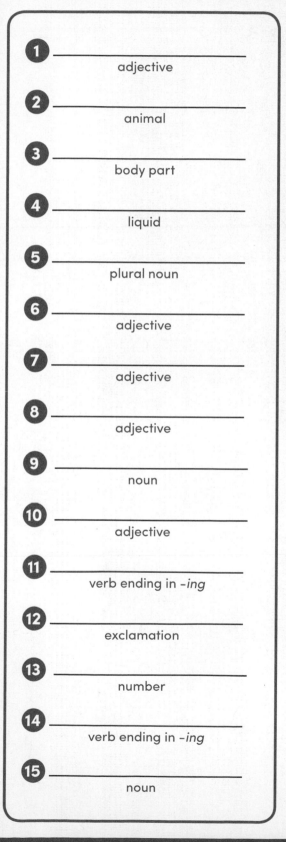

1 _____
  adjective

2 _____
  animal

3 _____
  body part

4 _____
  liquid

5 _____
  plural noun

6 _____
  adjective

7 _____
  adjective

8 _____
  adjective

9 _____
  noun

10 _____
  adjective

11 _____
  verb ending in *-ing*

12 _____
  exclamation

13 _____
  number

14 _____
  verb ending in *-ing*

15 _____
  noun

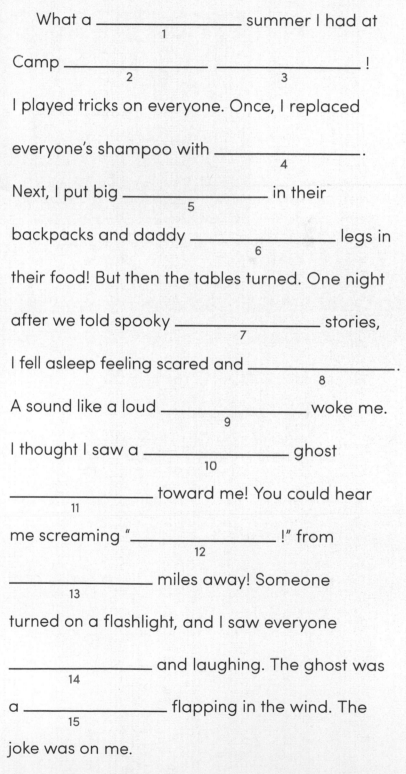

What a _____ summer I had at
           1

Camp _____ _____ !
         2   3

I played tricks on everyone. Once, I replaced

everyone's shampoo with _____.
                                    4

Next, I put big _____ in their
                        5

backpacks and daddy _____ legs in
                              6

their food! But then the tables turned. One night

after we told spooky _____ stories,
                              7

I fell asleep feeling scared and _____.
                                          8

A sound like a loud _____ woke me.
                             9

I thought I saw a _____ ghost
                          10

_____ toward me! You could hear
        11

me screaming "_____ !" from
                       12

_____ miles away! Someone
        13

turned on a flashlight, and I saw everyone

_____ and laughing. The ghost was
        14

a _____ flapping in the wind. The
         15

joke was on me.

Math's Got It Covered

Soccer players sure have a lot of ground to cover. Just how much exactly?
Answer the questions about the soccer field pictured below.
Figure out the answers in yards and then in feet.

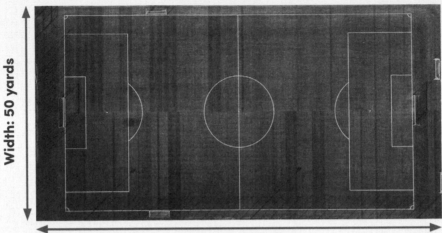

Width: 50 yards

Length: 100 yards

1 What is the length of the field? _____ yards | _____ feet

What is the width of the field? _____ yards | _____ feet

What is the perimeter of the field _____ yards | _____ feet

What is the area of the field? _____ yards | _____ feet

2 If you divide the field in half at the
halfway line, what is the perimeter then? _____ yards | _____ feet

What is the area? _____ yards | _____ feet

3 Imagine a field with a length of 130 yards and a width of 75 yards.

What is the perimeter of that field? _____

What is the area of that field? _____

The **perimeter** is the sum of the length of all sides of the shape.

The **area** of a shape is the number of square units needed to cover the shape.

Subject and Object Pronouns

A **subject pronoun**—*I, you, he, she, it, they,* or *we*—can replace the subject of a sentence.

An **object pronoun**—*me, you, him, her, it, us,* or *them*—can replace a noun that is the object of an action verb or that follows a preposition.

Choose the pronoun in parentheses that completes each sentence and write it on the line. Then identify the kind of pronoun it is by writing *S* for subject or *O* for object.

1 _____ took a boat trip through the Everglades. (We, Us)   _____

2 The boat's captain gave _____ a special tour. (we, us)   _____

3 The captain said, "_____ will love the wildlife here!" (You, Us)   _____

4 _____ brought my camera in my backpack. (I, Me)   _____

5 I used _____ to photograph birds, turtles, and an alligator. (he, it)   _____

6 My sister Kit carried paper and pencils with _____. (she, her)   _____

7 Kit used _____ to sketch scenes of the Everglades. (they, them)   _____

8 _____ is an excellent artist. (She, Her)   _____

Rewrite each sentence. Replace the underlined words with the correct subject or object pronoun.

9 <u>Our grandparents</u> sent a postcard to <u>my sister, my brother, and me</u>.

_____

10 <u>The postcard</u> was addressed to <u>my older brother</u>.

_____

More Fractions

Read the fraction.
Then shade the part of the whole shape that the fraction represents.

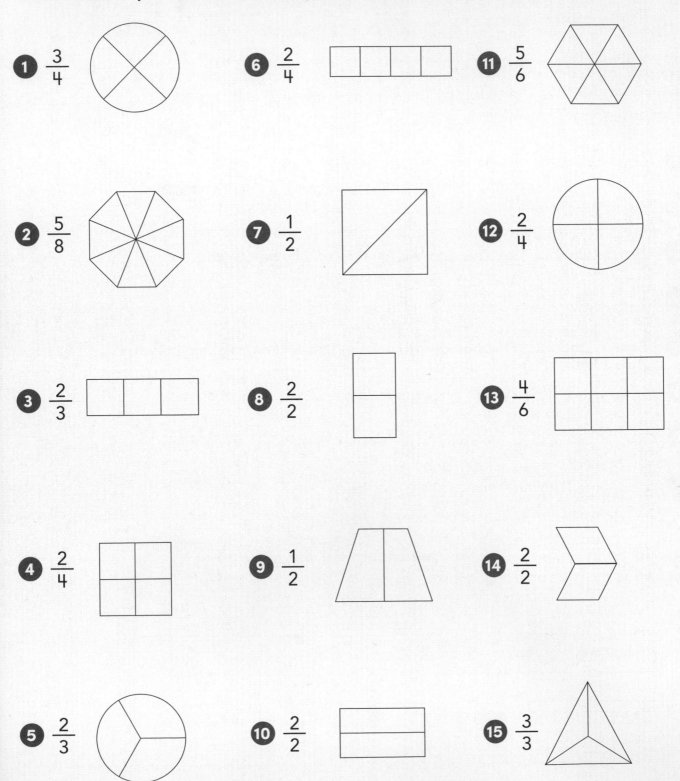

1 $\frac{3}{4}$

2 $\frac{5}{8}$

3 $\frac{2}{3}$

4 $\frac{2}{4}$

5 $\frac{2}{3}$

6 $\frac{2}{4}$

7 $\frac{1}{2}$

8 $\frac{2}{2}$

9 $\frac{1}{2}$

10 $\frac{2}{2}$

11 $\frac{5}{6}$

12 $\frac{2}{4}$

13 $\frac{4}{6}$

14 $\frac{2}{2}$

15 $\frac{3}{3}$

Here Comes the Sun

Do you like the sun? Here is a way to have a sun in your room every day!

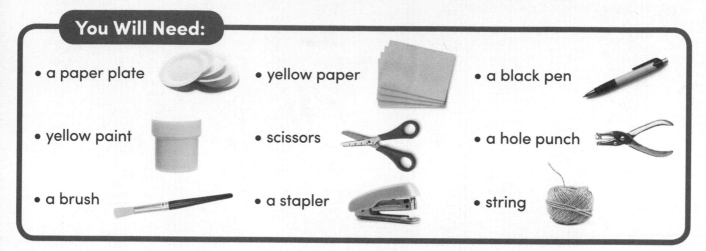

You Will Need:

- a paper plate
- yellow paper
- a black pen
- yellow paint
- scissors
- a hole punch
- a brush
- a stapler
- string

Step 1: Paint the back of the plate yellow.

Step 2: Put your hand on the yellow paper. Spread your fingers. Draw around your hand. Draw your hand 7 times.

Step 3: Cut out the 7 hands.

Step 4: Staple the hands around the plate.

Step 5: Draw a happy face on your sun.

Step 6: Make a hole at the top of the plate.

Step 7: Put string through the hole. Hang up the plate in your room!

1 What is the first thing you should do?

_____

2 What should you do after you draw your hand 7 times?

_____

3 What is Step 6?
- ◯ Make a hole at the top of the plate.
- ◯ Staple the hands to the plate.
- ◯ Draw a happy face on your sun.
- ◯ Cut out the 7 hands.

Multiplication

Rewrite each expression using the associative property.
The first two are done for you.

1 (3 x 2) x 7

$\qquad$ 6 x 7 $\qquad$

2 9 x (2 x 5)

$\qquad$ 9 x 10 $\qquad$

3 (3 x 2) x 5

4 (4 x 2) x 6

5 (2 x 5) x 7

6 (3 x 2) x 6

7 9 x (3 x 3)

8 6 x (2 x 5)

9 7 x (4 x 2)

10 4 x (4 x 2)

11 (2 x 4) x 6

12 (2 x 2) x 8

13 (2 x 2) x 9

14 (3 x 3) x 7

15 (2 x 3) x 9

Great Gardening Tips

Sentences can be combined to make them more interesting.
Key words can help put two sentences together. For example:

Old: *I will plan my garden. I am waiting for spring.*

New: *I will plan my garden while I am waiting for spring.*

Write a new sentence using the key words in each flower.

1 Fill a cup with water. Add some flower seeds. **and**

_____

2 Let them soak. They need to be softened. **because**

_____

3 Fill a cup with dirt. The seeds soak in water. **while**

_____

4 Bury the seeds in the cup. The dirt covers them. **until**

_____

5 Add water to the plant. Do not add too much water. **but**

_____

6 Set the cup in the sun. The plant will grow. **so**

_____

Fractions on a Number Line

Label the fractions on each number line. The first one is done for you.

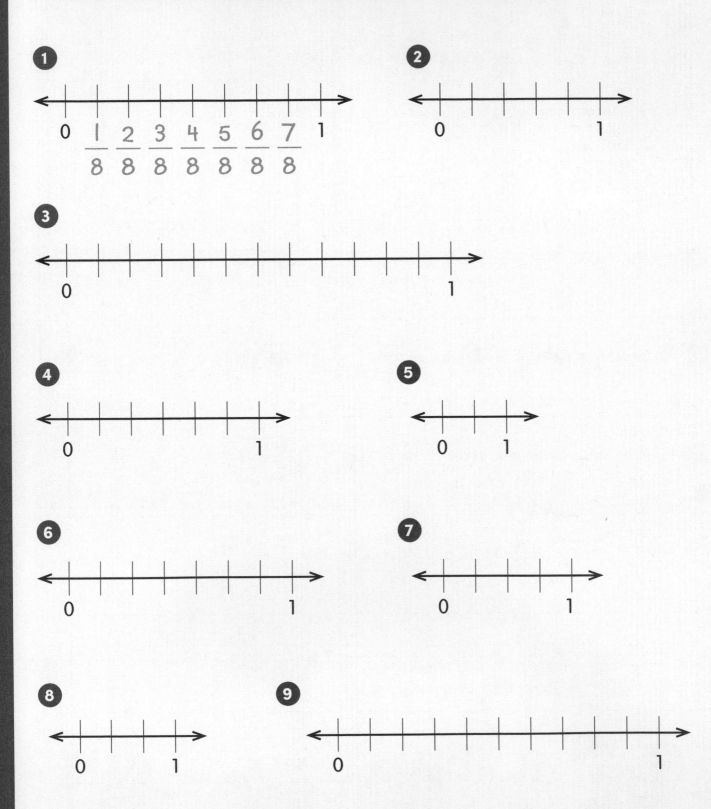

Two Poems

Read the poems. Then answer the questions.

Poem 1

Soon the night will fade away,

Darkness soon will change to day.

Time to rub your sleepy eyes

And stretch your legs, begin to rise.

Poem 2

Gold and purple beams

Sparkle in the early dawn.

Robins pipe delight.

1 What is the subject of each poem?

_____

2 How are the poems different?

_____

_____

3 Which poem do you prefer? Explain why.

_____

_____

_____

Flying With Fact Families

Write the multiplication and division sentences for each set of numbers.

The fact family for 5, 6, and 30 is:

$5 \times 6 = 30$ $30 \div 6 = 5$

$6 \times 5 = 30$ $30 \div 5 = 6$

1 2, 3, 6

_____

_____

_____

_____

2 3, 7, 21

_____

_____

_____

_____

3 3, 6, 18

_____

_____

_____

_____

4 6, 7, 42

_____

_____

_____

_____

5 7, 8, 56

_____

_____

_____

_____

6 6, 9, 54

_____

_____

_____

_____

7 5, 12, 60

_____

_____

_____

_____

8 8, 9, 72

_____

_____

_____

_____

9 9, 12, 108

_____

_____

_____

_____

10 11, 12, 132

_____

_____

_____

_____

11 4, 5, 20

_____

_____

_____

_____

12 5, 7, 35

_____

_____

_____

_____

Challenge

There are 4 families traveling together on an airplane. They need 24 seats in all. If each family has the same number of members, how many are in each family?

Help Your Child Get Ready: Week 10

Here are some activities that you and your child might enjoy.

Cartoon Flip Books

With a little bit of patience, your child can make his or her own cartoon flip book. Explain that in a cartoon, lots of images—one just slightly different from the last—are put together to make it appear as though a character is moving. Have your child draw a character on the last sheet of a small pad of paper. On the next sheet, have him or her draw the character just a bit above where the character last was. Have your child continue doing this until the entire act of jumping is illustrated. When he or she flips the pages of the book, the character will appear to be jumping.

Constellation Watch

Help your child identify a few constellations. Easy ones to start with are the Big Dipper and Orion. Then have him or her research other constellations and their names.

Family Coat of Arms

Have your child make a family coat of arms on a piece of poster board. Have him or her divide a shield shape into quadrants. In each quadrant, he or she can draw a symbol that represents one aspect of your family. Then proudly display your coat of arms.

Sign Your Name

Invite your child to learn how to spell his or her name in sign language. He or she can use an encyclopedia or go online to find the sign language alphabet.

These are the skills your child will be working on this week.

Math
- solve word problems using multiplication and division
- understand perimeter and area
- identify equal fractions on a number line
- make a bar graph

Reading
- main idea and details
- compare and contrast

Phonics & Vocabulary
- use temporal words and phrases

Grammar & Writing
- use quotation marks and punctuation
- parts of speech
- build a paragraph: closing sentences

Incentive Chart: Week 10

Week 10	Day 1	Day 2	Day 3	Day 4	Day 5
Put a sticker to show you completed each day's work.	☆ ☆	☆ ☆	☆ ☆	☆ ☆	☆ ☆

CONGRATULATIONS!

Wow! You did a great job this week!

This certificate is presented to:

_____

_____ _____
Date   Parent/Caregiver's Signature

Look Who's Talking

Quotation marks surround a character's exact words. In a statement, use a comma to separate the character's exact words from the rest of the sentence. In a question and an exclamation, use the correct ending punctuation after the character's exact words.

Statement: *"I have to go now,"* said my friend.

Question: *"Where are you?"* asked my mom.

Exclamation: *"Wow!"* the boy exclaimed.

Look at the pictures and read the speech bubbles below. Place what each child says in a sentence. Use quotation marks and correct punctuation. The above examples can help you.

Somebody turned out the lights!

_____

_____

What makes you think I've been eating cake?

_____

_____

_____

My parents finally let me get my ears pierced.

_____

_____

_____

Decision Time

Decide whether to multiply or divide. Solve.

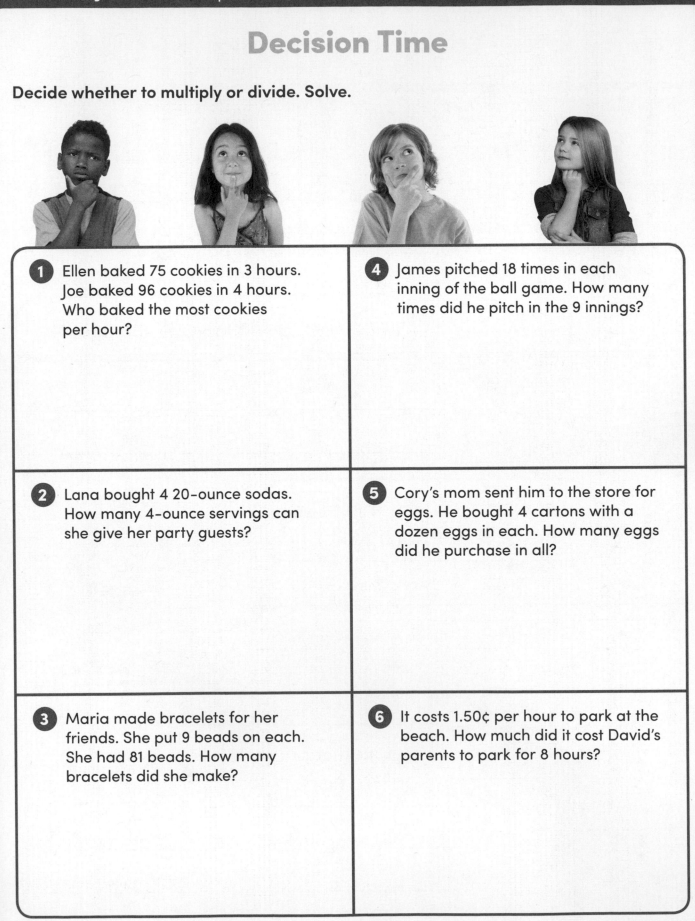

1 Ellen baked 75 cookies in 3 hours. Joe baked 96 cookies in 4 hours. Who baked the most cookies per hour?

4 James pitched 18 times in each inning of the ball game. How many times did he pitch in the 9 innings?

2 Lana bought 4 20-ounce sodas. How many 4-ounce servings can she give her party guests?

5 Cory's mom sent him to the store for eggs. He bought 4 cartons with a dozen eggs in each. How many eggs did he purchase in all?

3 Maria made bracelets for her friends. She put 9 beads on each. She had 81 beads. How many bracelets did she make?

6 It costs 1.50¢ per hour to park at the beach. How much did it cost David's parents to park for 8 hours?

Attack of the Massive Watermelon!

Don't read the story yet! Write a word for the parts of speech listed under the blanks on the left. Then write the words in the story and read the story aloud.

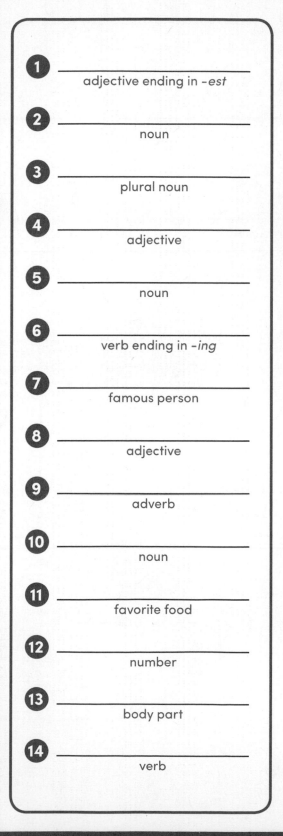

1 _____
adjective ending in *-est*

2 _____
noun

3 _____
plural noun

4 _____
adjective

5 _____
noun

6 _____
verb ending in *-ing*

7 _____
famous person

8 _____
adjective

9 _____
adverb

10 _____
noun

11 _____
favorite food

12 _____
number

13 _____
body part

14 _____
verb

I decided to grow the _____
1

garden in the world. I used a _____
2

to dig holes in the yard; then I spread seeds

and _____ all around. Soon, my
3

garden started looking _____ . I
4

had planted _____ seeds, but a
5

watermelon started _____ out of
6

the ground! This watermelon became bigger

than _____! Mom said we should
7

eat it before it turned _____ . So
8

every day I climbed _____ up a
9

_____ , then leaped to the top of
10

the melon and cut off huge pieces. We made

watermelon shakes, and _____ with
11

watermelon sauce. I've eaten almost nothing

but watermelon for the last _____
12

months! Mom said, "Don't look a gift horse in the

_____ ." I sure learned a lesson: *Don't*
13

bite off more than you can _____!
14

Mr. Knapp's Rug Shop

The **perimeter** is the distance around a figure. To find the perimeter, add together the length of the two sides and the width of the two sides.

The **area** of a figure is the number of square units inside a figure. The area of a figure can be found by multiplying the length times the width.

Mr. Knapp's rugs are too plain! Follow the directions below and help him by making his rugs much more attractive.

- Draw flowers on the rug with a perimeter of 26 feet.

- Draw a smiling face in the center of the rug with an area of 36 feet.

- Draw stripes on the rug with a perimeter of 20 feet.

- Draw a design of your choice on the rug with an area of 15 feet.

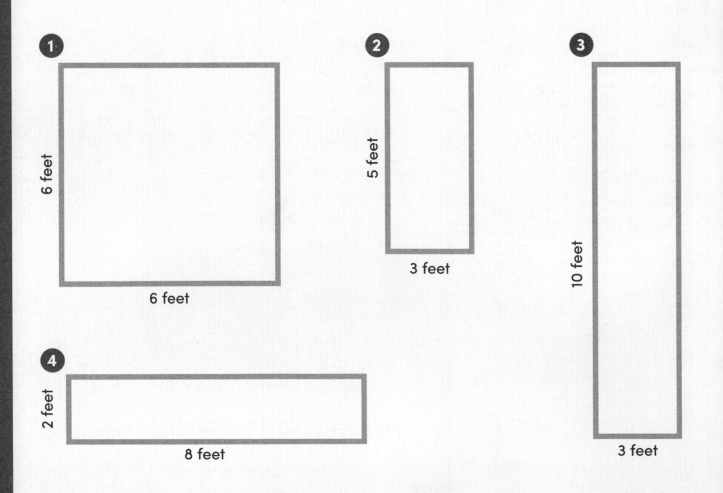

Sequence Words

Sequence is the order in which events happen. Words such as *now, then, when, soon, next, later, while, before,* and *after* help explain when an event happened in relation to another event. Writers use these sequence words to make their writing clear to readers.

Underline the sequence words in each sentence.

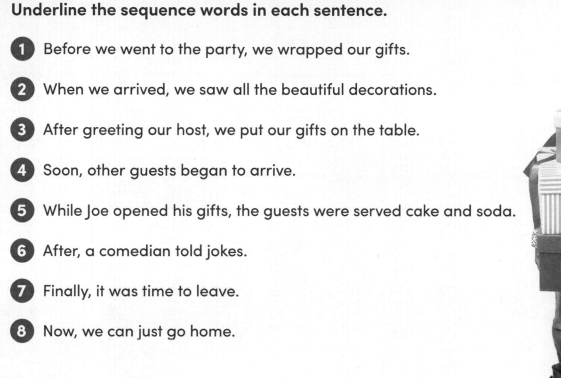

1 Before we went to the party, we wrapped our gifts.

2 When we arrived, we saw all the beautiful decorations.

3 After greeting our host, we put our gifts on the table.

4 Soon, other guests began to arrive.

5 While Joe opened his gifts, the guests were served cake and soda.

6 After, a comedian told jokes.

7 Finally, it was time to leave.

8 Now, we can just go home.

Choose words from the Word Bank to complete the story.

Word Bank

then	next	after	at last	first

Colleen was excited. _____ the day of the big volleyball match was

here! _____ a brief morning practice, the team ate breakfast together

and the coach sent them home to rest. Colleen took a short nap and called a

teammate to discuss strategy. _____, it was time to return to the gym.

_____, Colleen put on her kneepads, _____ she put on her

elbow pads. She was ready to go!

Equal Fractions

Two equal fractions are shown on each pair of number lines.
Write the equal fractions above the number lines. The first one is done for you.

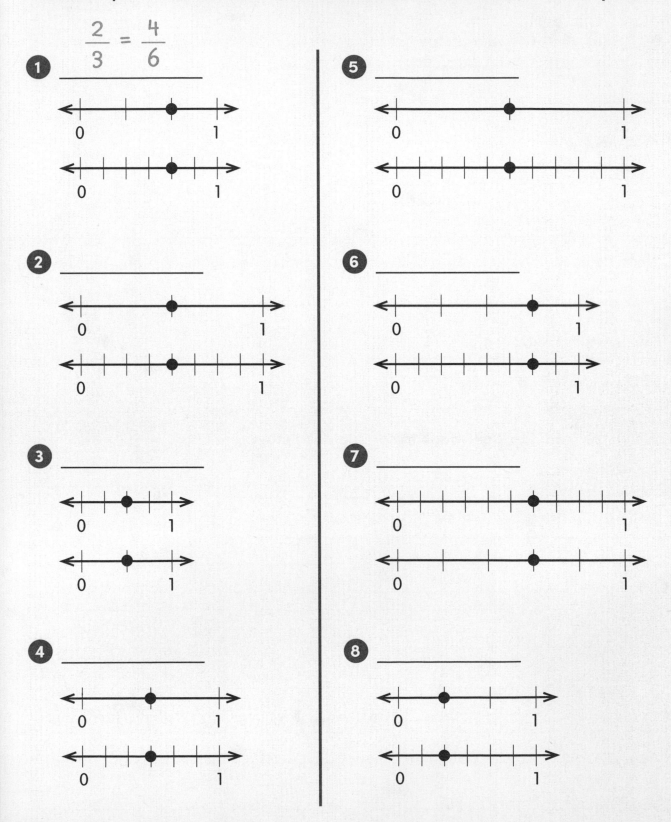

1 $\frac{2}{3} = \frac{4}{6}$

© Scholastic Inc.

Closing Time!

The last sentence in a paragraph is called the **closing sentence**.
It restates the topic sentence in a new way.

Find a closing sentence to match each topic sentence. Write the closing sentence.

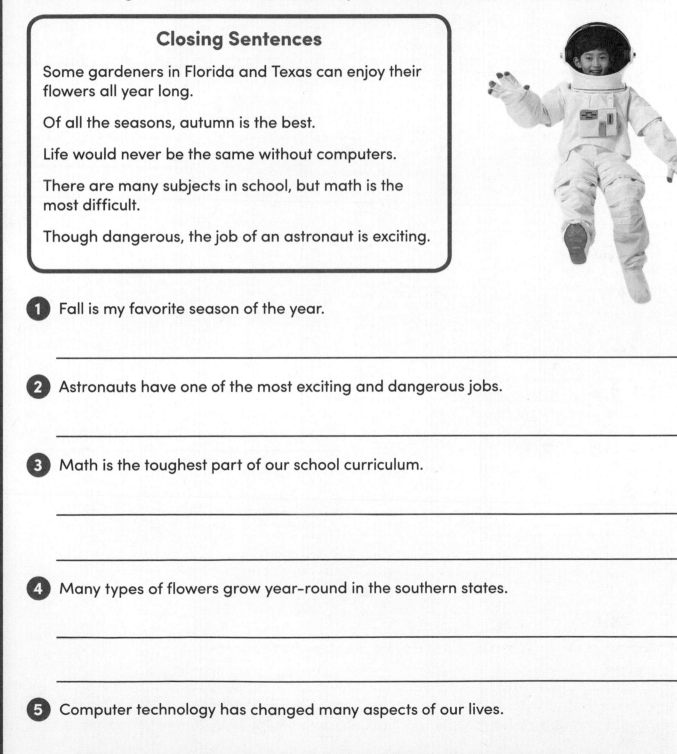

Closing Sentences

Some gardeners in Florida and Texas can enjoy their flowers all year long.

Of all the seasons, autumn is the best.

Life would never be the same without computers.

There are many subjects in school, but math is the most difficult.

Though dangerous, the job of an astronaut is exciting.

1 Fall is my favorite season of the year.

_____

2 Astronauts have one of the most exciting and dangerous jobs.

_____

3 Math is the toughest part of our school curriculum.

_____

_____

4 Many types of flowers grow year-round in the southern states.

_____

_____

5 Computer technology has changed many aspects of our lives.

_____

Quick Dry

Engineer David Hu wanted to determine how different mammals shake to dry off. He found that the smaller the animal, the faster it shook. He measured both the animals' shaking rates and the radius of their torsos (measured from behind the animal's shoulders). Hu found that there was a relationship between the animals' torso radius and the speed at which they shook.

Use the data in the chart about the animals' torso sizes to complete the blank bar graph. Make sure you give your graph a title and label the vertical and horizontal axes. Then answer the questions that follow.

Animal Torso Sizes	
Animal	**Radius** (centimeters)
Brown bear	24
Gulf Coast sheep	15
Kangaroo	8.1
Kunekune pig	13.3
Rat	2.6
River otter	5.5

Title:_____

Vertical axis:

Horizontal axis

1 Which animal has the smallest torso?

_____

2 How much larger is a Kunekune pig's torso than a river otter's torso?

_____

3 Which animal's torso is about three times the size of a kangaroo's?

_____

4 How does creating a bar graph from the data help you to interpret the information?

_____

This Plant Can Count!

Read the article. Then answer the questions.

Most plants get many of the important nutrients they need from soil. But not the Venus flytrap. It lives in parts of North and South Carolina where the soil doesn't have all the minerals it needs to grow. To survive, this **carnivorous** plant traps and eats insects. Now, scientists have learned a new detail about how it catches its prey. It counts!

A Venus flytrap has a special feature on its leaves called trigger hairs. When a bug touches them, the plant knows a meal is near. Scientists in Germany recently found out that the Venus flytrap counts how often its trigger hairs are touched. The first touch puts the plant on alert. The second touch causes it to close its trap. After five touches, the Venus flytrap makes special juices to **digest** the bug.

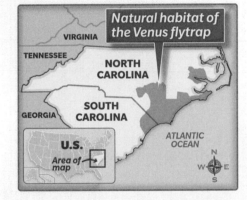

Scientist Rainer Hedrich says that counting helps the plant make sure that it has caught a meaty meal. A tiny bug or even a raindrop might touch the trigger hairs once or twice. But if the hairs are touched a lot, the plant knows that dinner is in its grip.

Words to Know

carnivorous: animal-eating

digest: break down food so that it can be used by the body

1 You can tell from the article that the job of a Venus flytrap's trigger hair is to _____.
- ○ make special juices
- ○ scare away insects
- ○ detect insects
- ○ collect raindrops

2 The photograph supports the article by showing how a Venus flytrap _____.
- ○ catches insects
- ○ gets nutrients from soil
- ○ counts to five
- ○ compares to other plants

3 Where is the Venus flytrap's natural habitat? _____

Trapped

In "This Plant Can Count!," on page 127, you read about how a Venus flytrap catches its meals. Below, compare the Venus flytrap to two other carnivorous plants. Then answer the questions.

Venus Flytrap

This plant's snap-trap is an open-and-shut case.

Ⓐ **Teeth:** These prevent animals from escaping the closed trap.

Ⓑ **Lobes:** A Venus flytrap's leaf is made up of two lobes that snap together over the victim.

Ⓒ **Trigger hairs:** Touching these causes the leaf to slam shut.

Sundew

The sundew's trap is a sticky affair.

Ⓐ **Tentacles:** Stalk-like features on the leaf move to catch insects.

Ⓑ **Gel-producing glands:** These produce a sticky liquid that attracts and traps prey.

Pitcher Plant

If an insect slips up, it likely won't make it out of this trap.

Ⓐ **Lid:** Some pitcher plants have lids that produce nectar to attract prey.

Ⓑ **Pitcher cup:** Victims fall into the liquid-filled cup and drown.

Ⓒ **Rim:** Insects are attracted to nectar here.

1 Which plant uses tentacles to catch its prey?

○ Venus flytrap   ○ pitcher plant   ○ sundew   ○ lobe

2 Which part of a pitcher plant catches the insects when they fall?

○ the lid   ○ the cup   ○ the rim   ○ the teeth

3 Which two plants attract insects by making a special liquid?

_____

4 Compare how a Venus flytrap catches a bug with how a pitcher plant traps one. What is one difference between them?

_____

_____

Answer Key

Week 1

The Case of Strange Playground Equipment

Build a roller coaster for the school playground? Find out what the Super-Riders Construction Team thinks about this highly unusual request!

Underline all the common nouns in the letter below. Then go back and circle the proper nouns.

Grammar Clues
A common noun names any person, place, or thing.
A proper noun names a particular person, place, or thing. A proper noun begins with a capital letter.

Dear Principal Billsley,

It's very unusual for my company to receive a letter like the one you sent. We've never built a roller coaster in a school's backyard before. We're thrilled for the opportunity!

The Super-Riders Construction Team has taken a look at the plans you included with your letter. It's a shame you used a crayon. The ideas you drew on the school picture were hard to read. But we liked what we saw. As you wrote, the second loop will require demolishing the school cook's cafeteria. I hope she won't mind.

Of course, every good roller coaster needs an exciting name. I'm not sure your suggestion, the Kara Has Cooties Coaster is appropriate. What about the Multiplication Shocker or the Research Report Terror? That's sure to get the kids excited.

One more thing: just between us, you should work on your spelling. And your signature looks like a kid wrote it!

I think this will certainly help Pickens Elementary with the three R's of a great education: reading, writing . . . and rides! If you ever think about expanding, let us know. We build great water parks.

Sincerely,
Tim Shouting, manager

11

Add Up!

Find the sum.

1. 25 + 15 = **40**
2. 72 + 18 = **90**
3. 306 + 624 = **930**
4. 308 + 296 = **604**
5. 186 + 321 = **507**
6. 62 + 71 = **133**
7. 71 + 54 = **125**
8. 518 + 137 = **655**
9. 738 + 951 = **1,689**
10. 715 + 839 = **1,554**
11. 54 + 26 = **80**
12. 67 + 14 = **81**
13. 763 + 807 = **1,570**
14. 645 + 237 = **882**
15. 204 + 599 = **803**

12

Buckets of Fun

An adjective describes a noun. Adjectives help you imagine how something looks, feels, smells, sounds, or tastes.

Write three describing words on each bucket to fit the bucket's category.

Answers will vary.

words that describe size
words that describe taste or smell
words that describe sounds
words that describe how something feels
words that describe weather
words that describe feelings

13

Climbing to the Top

Multiply.

1. 9 x 6 = **54**, 8 x 9 = **72**, 8 x 5 = **40**, 8 x 6 = **48**, 8 x 3 = **24**
2. 9 x 3 = **27**, 9 x 9 = **81**, 7 x 8 = **56**, 2 x 9 = **18**, 4 x 8 = **32**
3. 9 x 8 = **72**, 9 x 0 = **0**, 2 x 8 = **16**, 8 x 8 = **64**, 6 x 9 = **54**
4. 9 x 4 = **36**, 9 x 7 = **63**, 1 x 9 = **9**, 8 x 4 = **32**, 0 x 8 = **0**
5. 3 x 9 = **27**, 5 x 8 = **40**, 7 x 9 = **63**, 1 x 8 = **8**, 5 x 9 = **45**

14

What Do You Do With It?

Each word in bold below names something. Do you know what to do with each item? Underline the most likely answer. Use a dictionary to check your answers.

1. A **beret** is _____.
   a dance step / prepared for breakfast / worn on your head
2. A **couch** is _____.
   a place to sit / a place to ride / something to paint
3. A **viola** is _____.
   planted in a garden / used to play ball / heard in an orchestra
4. A **microscope** is _____.
   used to hear sounds / used to measure / used to observe cells
5. A **novel** is _____.
   watched / read / watered
6. A **ballot** is _____.
   used to cast a vote / used to play a game / barbecued
7. **Moccasins** are _____.
   eaten / used to write / put on your feet
8. A **biscuit** is _____.
   thrown / mashed / eaten
9. A **spatula** is _____.
   served for dessert / used to flip pancakes / used to float
10. A **ballet** is _____.
   used to hammer / danced on a stage / put in an aquarium

If you come across an unfamiliar word, try to guess its meaning using context clues and what you know about word parts. Then look it up in a dictionary.

15

Take It Away!

Find the difference.

1. 83 - 6 = **77**
2. 61 - 34 = **27**
3. 65 - 36 = **29**
4. 231 - 108 = **123**
5. 614 - 295 = **319**
6. 71 - 8 = **63**
7. 82 - 56 = **26**
8. 84 - 29 = **55**
9. 774 - 226 = **548**
10. 832 - 597 = **235**
11. 34 - 5 = **29**
12. 31 - 14 = **17**
13. 92 - 59 = **33**
14. 541 - 323 = **218**
15. 964 - 188 = **776**

16

Rock Your World

A telling sentence is called a statement. A statement begins with a capital letter and ends with a period.

Read the paragraph.
Find the three statements that are missing a capital letter and a period.
Then rewrite the three statements correctly on the lines below.

Rocks

There are three types of rocks. one type is called igneous These are rocks that were made by volcanoes. Another kind is called sedimentary. they are formed by layers of rocks, plants, and animals The last type of rock is called metamorphic. They are rocks that change because of heat and pressure. rocks are found everywhere in our world

1. **One type is called igneous.**
2. **They are formed by layers of rocks, plants, and animals.**
3. **Rocks are found everywhere in our world.**

17

Rounding to Tens

Round each value to the nearest 10.
Draw a line to match each answer on the left with one on the right.

LEFT | RIGHT
1. 18 = **20**   A. 74 = **70**
2. 31 = **30**   B. 88 = **90**
3. 14 = **10**   C. 15 = **20**
4. 65 = **70**   D. 53 = **50**
5. 47 = **50**   E. 8 = **10**
6. 91 = **90**   F. 26 = **30**

Challenge
Round the answer of 9 x 8 to the nearest 10. **70** Circle the answers that match above.

18

130

Boot Fruit

Read the story. Then answer the questions.

When Rupert planted a boot in his garden, his neighbors made fun of him. It was early spring—the normal planting time. But a boot? "Poor Rupert must be **daft**," they whispered. But Rupert cheerfully cared for his boot every day. He sang to the boot plant as he weeded, watered, and watched. As it grew, so did everyone's wonder. By fall, Rupert stood beside a small tree. He loved the little green fruit that hung in pairs. "Boot fruit!" he said proudly. "Bring your children around in a few weeks to try them on. I'll give free fresh boots for any feet they fit!" Free boots from a tree? Some neighbors still gossiped, but the word spread. Soon, parents brought their children to try on the home-grown boots, which were no longer green. Now they were many different colors. Rupert handed out free fruit boots, as promised. How do you think next year's crop will turn out?

1. What is another word for **daft**?
   ○ clever
   ○ cold
   ● crazy

2. Why would Rupert give away boot fruits?
   ● to show his kind heart
   ○ because they were too small for his feet
   ○ to earn money before the winter set in

3. What can you tell about the boot fruit from the picture?
   Answers will vary.

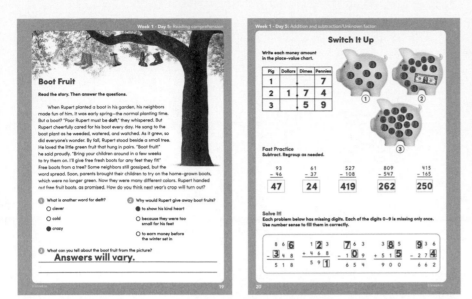

Switch It Up

Write each money amount in the place-value chart.

Pig	Dollars	Dimes	Pennies
1			7
2	1	7	4
3		5	9

Fast Practice
Subtract. Regroup as needed.

93 − 46	61 − 37	527 − 108	809 − 547	415 − 165
47	**24**	**419**	**262**	**250**

Solve It!
Each problem below has missing digits. Each of the digits 0–9 is missing only once. Use number sense to fill them in correctly.

```
  8 6 6      1 2 3      7 6 3      3 8 5      9 3 6
- 3 4 8    + 4 6 8    - 1 0 9    + 5 1 5    - 2 7 4
  5 1 8      5 9 1      6 5 4      9 0 0      6 6 2
```

Week 2

The Case of the Frog Prince

Ever since Prince Leonardo was turned into a frog, his spelling skills have really suffered. His letter below is filled with spelling errors. Can you help him?

Circle each misspelled word. Then write down the correct spelling in the spaces provided.
Hint: There are 20 misspelled words.

Dear Madam Witch,

I am writting to you to tell you how disssapointed am that you have refussed a terrm me back into a prince. I have apologizd over and over agian for making that little coment about the wart on your nose. I have suffered enough. If you don't think so, turn yourself into a frog and see what it is like. I must share my pond with three verry nasty geese. The pond water is wrecking my skin. And the food is terrible althou I did catch a most delishouly yesterday for lunch. I miss my palase.

In your last letter, you told me that the spell will be broken when a princess gives me a kiss. I am afraid that there is a real shortage of princesses around the kingdom. Most are off at collige. If a princess did happen to see me at the pond, I somehow dout she would want to kiss me.

Please, won't you reconsider? You know wear to find me: on the second rock to the rite.

Sincerely,
Prince Leonardo
(the geese call me Prince Slimo)

P.S. If you turn me back into a prince, I'll pay the finest doctor to take care of that little problem in your nasal area.

1. writing
2. disappointed
3. refused
4. turn
5. apologized
6. again
7. comment
8. enough
9. very
10. wrecking
11. terrible
12. although
13. delicious
14. palace
15. afraid
16. college
17. doubt
18. reconsider
19. where
20. right

Find the Patterns

What is the pattern for the numbers 0, 2, 4, 6, 8, 10, 12, 14, 16, 18?
The pattern shows multiples of 2.

Complete each pattern.

1. 3, 6, 9, 12, **15**, **18**, **21**, **24**, **27**
2. 4, 8, 12, 16, **20**, **24**, **28**, **32**, **36**
3. 1, 2, 3, 4, **5**, **6**, **7**, **8**, **9**
4. 7, 14, 21, **28**, **35**, **42**, **49**, **56**
5. 10, 20, 30, **40**, **50**, **60**, **70**, **80**
6. **9**, 18, 27, **36**, **45**, **54**, **63**
7. 6, 12, **18**, **24**, 30, **36**, **42**, **48**
8. **11**, **22**, **33**, 44, **55**, **66**, 77
9. 5, 10, 15, **20**, **25**, **30**, **35**, **40**
10. 8, **16**, 24, **32**, 40, **48**, **56**, **64**
11. 10, 12, 14, **16**, **18**, **20**, **22**, **24**, **26**
12. **12**, 24, **36**, 48, 60, **72**, **84**, **96**, **108**

Three Nests

You can use **adjectives** to compare things. To compare two things, add **-er** to the adjective. To compare three or more things, add **-est**.

Biddie Bird has a friend named Betty. Betty always wants to outdo Biddie. If Biddie has a **clean** nest, Betty has a **cleaner** nest. Biddie and Betty have another friend named Birdie. She likes to outdo both Biddie and Betty. So she has the **cleanest** nest.

Read the sentences below. Then fill in the chart so the correct form of each adjective is under each bird's name.

	Biddie	Betty	Birdie
	clean	cleaner	cleanest
1	new	newer	newest
2	small	smaller	smallest
3	warm	warmer	warmest
4	round	rounder	roundest
5	neat	neater	neatest
6	soft	softer	softest

1. Betty's nest is **newer** than Biddie's.
2. Biddie has a **small** nest.
3. Birdie has the **warmest** nest of all.
4. Biddie's nest is **round**.
5. Birdie built the **neatest** nest.
6. Betty has a **softer** nest than Biddie.

It's All Relative

Remember that multiplication and division are related. Multiplying the quotient by the divisor will tell you the dividend.

Hi! Aren't we related?

You bet! When you multiply us, our product is the missing dividend!

Write each missing dividend.

1. **63** ÷ 9 = 7   **24** ÷ 4 = 6   **36** ÷ 6 = 6   **35** ÷ 5 = 7
2. **9** ÷ 3 = 3   **18** ÷ 2 = 9   **48** ÷ 8 = 6   **81** ÷ 9 = 9
3. **32** ÷ 4 = 8   **21** ÷ 3 = 7   **16** ÷ 2 = 8   **18** ÷ 3 = 6
4. **64** ÷ 8 = 8   **9** ÷ 1 = 9   **30** ÷ 5 = 6   **7** ÷ 7 = 1
5. **160** ÷ 4 = 40   **90** ÷ 3 = 30   **300** ÷ 3 = 100
6. **420** ÷ 7 = 60   **300** ÷ 5 = 60   **80** ÷ 2 = 40

Are we missing?

Who Won the Prize?

Personal pronouns are words used in place of nouns.
For example: *Katie* finished *her* chores and then *she* went out to play.
She (pronoun) takes the place of *Katie* (proper noun).

Personal Pronouns
I   me   you   he   him   she   her   it   we   us   they   them

Underline the personal pronouns in each sentence below.

1. Greg read the book and returned **it** to the library.
2. The teacher chose Lisa and **me** to hand out the papers.
3. **You** will represent the school at the spelling bee.
4. Did **I** receive a phone call?
5. Steven, please help **him** with the math homework.
6. All of **us** will be attending the football game.
7. Who will help **them** finish the decorations?
8. Tell **her** that **she** won the prize.
9. **We** will have to drive **him** to the party.
10. Please hang **it** up on the back wall.
11. How many of **you** will be able to attend?
12. Only four of **us** ate lunch in the cafeteria.

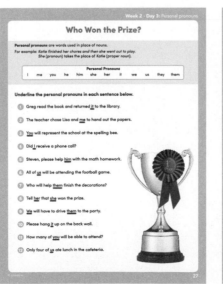

Division Decoder

Find each quotient.

1. 8 ÷ 2 = **4**
2. 10 ÷ 5 = **2**
3. 24 ÷ 4 = **6**
4. 50 ÷ 10 = **5**
5. 72 ÷ 9 = **8**
6. 32 ÷ 10 = **3 R2**
7. 48 ÷ 7 = **6 R6**
8. 29 ÷ 3 = **9 R2**
9. 65 ÷ 8 = **8 R1**
10. 92 ÷ 6 = **15 R2**

Decoder

1	F
2	E
2 remainder 2	D
3 remainder 2	L
4	R
5	U
6 remainder 6	I
7	W
7 remainder 6	N
8	I
9 remainder 1	S
9	A
9 remainder 2	T
10	C
11	C
15 remainder 2	P
15 remainder 3	I

Find the letter for each question's answer in the decoder. Write it in the blank spaces below to find the answer to the riddle.

What kind of tools do you use for math?

"M U L T I" P L I E R S
3 1 8 5 10 6 7 2 4 9

The Sunny Sahara

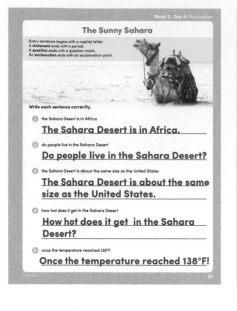

Every sentence begins with a capital letter.
A **statement** ends with a period.
A **question** ends with a question mark.
An **exclamation** ends with an exclamation point.

Write each sentence correctly.

1. the Sahara Desert is in Africa

The Sahara Desert is in Africa.

2. do people live in the Sahara Desert

Do people live in the Sahara Desert?

3. the Sahara Desert is about the same size as the United States

The Sahara Desert is about the same size as the United States.

4. how hot does it get in the Sahara Desert

How hot does it get in the Sahara Desert?

5. once the temperature reached 138°F

Once the temperature reached 138°F!

A Math Laugh

Circle the answer to each question.

Length

1. Which of these is the most likely measurement for the height of a door?
   C 3 feet   D 50 feet   (E 7 feet)

2. Which of these should be used to measure the height of a building?
   (A feet)   B inches   C miles

3. Which of these is the most likely height of a giraffe?
   H 15 inches   (I 15 feet)   J 15 yards

Capacity

4. Which of these should be used to measure the amount of water in a swimming pool?
   B quarts   (C gallons)   D ounces

5. Which of these is the smallest unit of measurement?
   C gallon   (D pint)   E quart

6. Which of these is the most likely amount in a glass of milk?
   P 25 cups   Q 1 quart   (R 8 ounces)

Weight

7. Which of these has a weight that should be measured in pounds?
   S a feather   (T a human baby)   U a grape

8. Which of these is the most likely weight of an elephant?
   C 4 pounds   (D 4 tons)   S 4 ounces

How do you charge a battery?
To find out, write the answer's letter above each question number.

With a C R E D I T   C A R D
       3 5 1 7 6 8   3 4 2 8

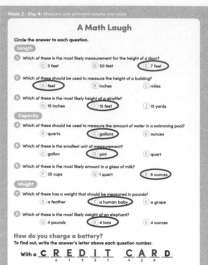

Talk With Your Hands

Some people can't hear. These people have a special way of talking. They talk with their hands. This is called "signing." There are two main ways to sign. First, you can spell out each letter in a word. Here is the word love.

Spelling words takes a long time. There is a faster way to sign. You can show a whole word with one sign.

To sign some words, you keep your hands still. (Look at the signs for love and ball below.) To sign other words, you need to move your hands. To sign the word dog, you pat your leg.

Signing is lots of fun. Anyone can learn. You can learn from a book. You can learn from a teacher. You can learn from a friend who uses signing every day. Here are good signs to start with:

love   ball   hello

Talk With Your Hands (continued)

1. What is this passage mostly about?
   ○ how to be a better speller
   ○ why some people cannot hear
   ○ all the things you can do with your hands
   ● using your hands to talk

2. Look at the sign. What letter is it?
   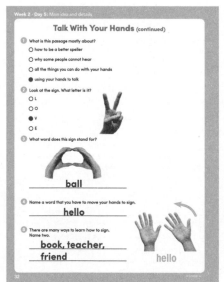
   ○ L
   ○ O
   ● V
   ○ E

3. What word does this sign stand for?

   ball

4. Name a word that you have to move your hands to sign.

   hello

5. There are many ways to learn how to sign. Name two.

   book, teacher, friend

   hello

Week 3

Prefixes

A **prefix** is a word part that is added to the beginning of a word.
A prefix changes the meaning of a word.

| mis- means "badly" | in- and un- mean "not" | sub- means "under" | re- means "again" |

A. Underline the prefix in each word below.
Write the number of the word next to its definition on the right.

1. **mis**behave — **6** not able
2. **mis**trust — **3** not said or done in a direct way
3. **in**direct — **7** a title that comes after the main title
4. **in**formal — **2** a feeling that someone cannot be trusted
5. **un**equal — **4** not formal, such as clothes or language
6. **un**able — **1** to behave or act badly
7. **sub**title — **5** not equal
8. **sub**total — **8** not the whole total
9. **re**count — **10** to come to or go to a place again
10. **re**turn — **9** to count again

B. Use the meaning in parentheses to add a prefix to each word to form a new word.

1. (again) **re** use   4. (not) **un** fair
2. (under) **sub** marine   5. (badly) **mis** lead
3. (not) **in** complete   6. (again) **re** start

C. Write a heading that tells how the words in each group are alike.

1. Prefix **in-**
   indirect
   incorrect
   insecure

2. Prefix **mis-**
   misname
   mistrust
   miscast

3. Prefix **un-**
   unfair
   unzip
   unfold

4. Prefix **re-**
   recount
   renew
   redo

Riddle and Review

In a multiplication problem, the numbers being multiplied are called **factors**. The answer is called the **product**.

Why did the math teacher choose multiplication to help his class grow?

To find out, multiply. Use the code to write the letter of each multiplication sentence on the blank above its product.

A 3 x 12 = **36**   H 2 x 9 = **18**   O 3 x 7 = **21**   U 2 x 12 = **24**
B 5 x 10 = **50**   I 4 x 7 = **28**   P 1 x 0 = **0**   W 5 x 5 = **25**
D 2 x 8 = **16**   L 5 x 6 = **30**   R 2 x 11 = **22**   Y 4 x 12 = **48**
E 4 x 11 = **44**   M 4 x 8 = **32**   S 5 x 7 = **35**   J 3 x 3 = **9**
G 2 x 6 = **12**   H 3 x 9 = **27**   T 5 x 9 = **45**

S O   T H A T   H I S   G R O U P
35 21 9 36 44 9 36 27 35 12 21 24 28 22

W O U L D   B E G I N   T O
25 21 24 30 16 50 44 12 27 18 9 21

G E T   L A R G E R
12 44 45 30 36 22 12 44 22

A N D
36 27 16

M U L T I P L Y!
32 24 30 45 28 0 30 48

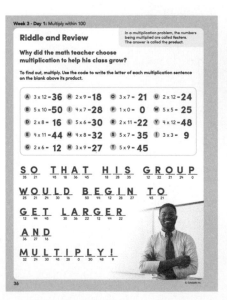

Irregular Plurals

Word Bank

| grandchildren | halves | mice | oxen | feet |
| heroes | geese | mysteries | sketches | sheep |

A. Use what you know. Choose a word from the Word Bank to complete each sentence.

1. The artist made **sketches** before beginning to paint.
2. A team of **oxen** pulled the hay wagon.
3. The grandparents called their **grandchildren** every week.
4. In the fall, wild **geese** fly south.
5. The **sheep** provided the farmer with all the wool she needed.
6. Many people like to read **mysteries**.
7. Abraham Lincoln is one of my **heroes**.
8. Molly cut the apple into **halves**.
9. The cat chased two **mice** but caught only one.
10. Sam put his **feet** into his new boots.

B. Read each question. Choose the best answer.

1. How do you make sketches?   □ write   ⊠ draw
2. Which word means "two"?   ⊠ halves   □ whole
3. Which could be a flock?   □ goose   ⊠ geese

Challenge
On another sheet of paper, write three sentences. Use at least one word from the Word Bank in each sentence.

A Ray of Fun

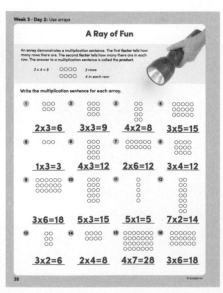

An **array** demonstrates a multiplication sentence. The first factor tells how many rows there are. The second factor tells how many there are in each row. The answer to a multiplication sentence is called the **product**.

2 x 4 = 8   OOOO 2 rows
            OOOO 4 in each row

Write the multiplication sentence for each array.

1. **2x3=6**   2. **3x3=9**   3. **4x2=8**   4. **3x5=15**

5. **1x3=3**   6. **4x3=12**   7. **2x6=12**   8. **3x4=12**

9. **3x6=18**   10. **5x3=15**   11. **5x1=5**   12. **7x2=14**

13. **3x2=6**   14. **2x4=8**   15. **4x7=28**   16. **3x6=18**

The Tallest Trees

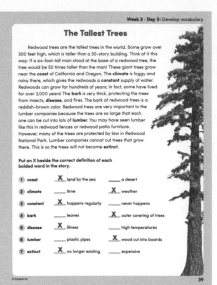

Redwood trees are the tallest trees in the world. Some grow over 300 feet high, which is taller than a 30-story building. Think of it this way: If a six-foot-tall man stood at the base of a redwood tree, the tree would be 50 times taller than the man! These giant trees grow near the **coast** of California and Oregon. The **climate** is foggy and rainy there, which gives the redwoods a **constant** supply of water. Redwoods can grow for hundreds of years; in fact, some have lived for over 2,000 years! The **bark** is very thick, protecting the trees from insects, **disease**, and fires. The bark of redwood trees is a reddish-brown color. Redwood trees are very important to the lumber companies because the trees are so large that each one can be cut into lots of **lumber**. You may have seen lumber like this in redwood fences or redwood patio furniture. However, many of the trees are protected by law in Redwood National Park. Lumber companies cannot cut trees that grow there. This is so the trees will not become **extinct**.

Put an X beside the correct definition of each bolded word in the story.

1. coast   **X** land by the sea   ___ a desert
2. climate   ___ time   **X** weather
3. constant   **X** happens regularly   ___ never happens
4. bark   ___ leaves   **X** outer covering of trees
5. disease   **X** illness   ___ high temperatures
6. lumber   ___ plastic pipes   **X** wood cut into boards
7. extinct   **X** no longer existing   ___ expensive

Find the Unknown

Use the multiplication chart to write the missing number for each equation below.

x	1	2	3	4	5	6	7	8	9	10
1	1	2	3	4	5	6	7	8	9	10
2	2	4	6	8	10	12	14	16	18	20
3	3	6	9	12	15	18	21	24	27	30
4	4	8	12	16	20	24	28	32	36	40
5	5	10	15	20	25	30	35	40	45	50
6	6	12	18	24	30	36	42	48	54	60
7	7	14	21	28	35	42	49	56	63	70
8	8	16	24	32	40	48	56	64	72	80
9	9	18	27	36	45	54	63	72	81	90
10	10	20	30	40	50	60	70	80	90	100

1. $24 \div 3 = $ **8**
2. $42 \div$ **7** $= 6$
3. $8 \times 7 = $ **56**
4. **4** $\times 8 = 32$
5. $48 \div 8 = $ **6**

6. $8 \times 9 = $ **72**
7. $5 \times$ **9** $= 45$
8. $54 \div$ **9** $= 6$
9. $3 \times 3 = $ **9**
10. $28 \div$ **4** $= 7$

11. ___ $3 \times 7 = 21$
12. **30** $\div 6 = 5$
13. $3 \times$ **9** $= 27$
14. $21 \div 7 = $ **3**
15. **6** $\times 3 = 18$

Missing Topics

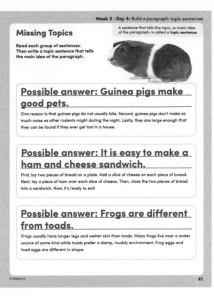

Read each group of sentences. Then write a topic sentence that tells the main idea of the paragraph.

> A sentence that tells the topic, or main idea of the paragraph, is called a topic sentence.

__Possible answer: Guinea pigs make good pets.__

One reason is that guinea pigs do not usually bite. Second, guinea pigs don't make as much noise as other rodents might during the night. Lastly, they are large enough that they can be found if they ever get lost in a house.

__Possible answer: It is easy to make a ham and cheese sandwich.__

First, lay two pieces of bread on a plate. Add a slice of cheese on each piece of bread. Next, lay a piece of ham over each slice of cheese. Then, close the two pieces of bread into a sandwich. Now, it's ready to eat!

__Possible answer: Frogs are different from toads.__

Frogs usually have longer legs and wetter skin than toads. Many frogs live near a water source of some kind while toads prefer a damp, muddy environment. Frog eggs and toad eggs are different in shape.

The Case of the Missing Factors

Complete the multiplication chart.

x	0	1	2	3	4	5	6	7	8	9
0	0	0	0	0	0	0	0	0	0	0
1	0	1	2	3	4	5	6	7	8	9
2	0	2	4	6	8	10	12	14	16	18
3	0	3	6	9	12	15	18	21	24	27
4	0	4	8	12	16	20	24	28	32	36
5	0	5	10	15	20	25	30	35	40	45
6	0	6	12	18	24	30	36	42	48	54
7	0	7	14	21	28	35	42	49	56	63
8	0	8	16	24	32	40	48	56	64	72
9	0	9	18	27	36	45	54	63	72	81

Use the chart to help Detective Dan find each missing factor.

1. $4 \times$ **3** $= 12$ $7 \times$ **2** $= 14$ $3 \times$ **9** $= 27$
2. $5 \times$ **6** $= 30$ $6 \times$ **6** $= 36$ $8 \times$ **8** $= 64$
3. **9** $\times 4 = 36$ **8** $\times 3 = 24$ **2** $\times 9 = 18$
4. **7** $\times 8 = 56$ **9** $\times 9 = 81$ **6** $\times 1 = 6$
5. $9 \times$ **5** $= 45$ **7** $\times 9 = 63$ $3 \times$ **8** $= 24$

The Crow and the Pitcher
Based on a Fable by Aesop

What is the crow's problem, and how does she solve it?

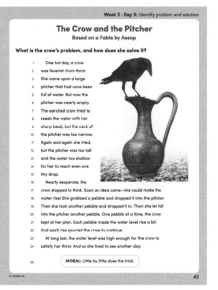

1. One hot day, a crow
2. was feverish from thirst.
3. She came upon a large
4. pitcher that had once been
5. full of water. But now the
6. pitcher was nearly empty.
7. The parched crow tried to
8. reach the water with her
9. sharp beak, but the neck of
10. the pitcher was too narrow.
11. Again and again she tried,
12. but the pitcher was too tall
13. and the water too shallow
14. for her to reach even one
15. tiny drop.
16. Nearly desperate, the
17. crow stopped to think. Soon an idea came—she could make the
18. water rise! She grabbed a pebble and dropped it into the pitcher.
19. Then she took another pebble and dropped it. Then she let fall
20. into the pitcher another pebble. One pebble at a time, the crow
21. kept at her plan. Each pebble made the water level rise a bit.
22. And each rise spurred the crow to continue.
23. At long last, the water level was high enough for the crow to
24. satisfy her thirst. And so she lived to see another day.
25.

> **MORAL:** Little by little does the trick.

The Crow and the Pitcher (continued)
Possible answers shown.

Answer each question. Give evidence from the fable.

1. If you feel **parched** (line 7), you would probably want ___
   - ○ something to eat
   - ● something to drink
   - ○ somewhere to sit
   - ○ someone to play with

   How did you pick your answer? **I read that the crow was feverish from thirst (lines 1–2).**

2. Which part of the pitcher is the neck (line 9)?
   - ○ its base
   - ○ its height
   - ○ its handle
   - ● its thinnest part

   What in the text helped you answer? **I reread lines 7-10. I also looked at the picture and saw the place on the pitcher that was too small for the crow's head to pass through to reach the water at the bottom.**

3. Explain the crow's problem. **The crow is very thirsty and finds some water, but she can't reach the water (lines 7–15).**

4. How do the pebbles make the water rise? **The heavy pebbles fall to the bottom and take up space, and lift the water up (lines 18–24).**

5. Explain the meaning of the moral in your own words. **Sometimes the way to solve a big problem is to take small steps.**

Week 4

The Root of the Matter

A word can have different parts. Many words have a main part, or **root**. The root contains the basic meaning of the word. For example, *ped* is the root in the word *pedal*. The meaning of *ped* is "foot." Feet are used to push down on the pedals of a bicycle to cause it to move.

The root is missing from a word in each sentence below. Use context clues and the meaning of the roots in the box to figure out the missing word part. Then write it in the space to complete the word.

pos = place	phon = sound	photo = light
port = carry	pop = people	

1. The **pop**ulation of our town is just over 20,000.
2. The orchestra will perform a sym**phon**y by Beethoven.
3. The **pos**ition of the hour hand shows that it is 2:00 P.M.
4. What goods does our country ex**port** to other countries?
5. During **photo**synthesis, plants use sunlight to make food.

List the words you completed. Then write your own definition for each word. Use a dictionary if you are not sure.

6. _____ **Answers will vary.**
7. _____
8. _____
9. _____
10. _____

Challenge

What other words do you know with the roots *ped, pos, phon, photo, port,* and *pop*? On another sheet of paper, write a word containing each root.

What gives milk, says "moo," and makes wishes come true?

Find the missing factor or dividend. Solve the riddle using your answers below.

11 / D $\times 2 = 22$	$4\overline{)20}$ = **5** E
12 / G $\times 7 = 84$	$2\overline{)4}$ = **2** A
9 / H $\times 4 = 36$	$3\overline{)18}$ = **6** N
8 / I $\times 3 = 24$	**7** / O $\div 1 = 7$
5 / M $\times 2 = 10$	**48** / Y $\div 4 = 12$
6 / R $\times 3 = 18$	**3** / T $\div 1 = 3$

Solve the Riddle!

Write the letter that goes with each number.

A D A I R Y
4 7 11 5 7 3

G O D M O T H E R
12 7 11 5 7 3 20 6

The Case of the Bumbling Cupids

Big Boss Cupid wrote this memo to America's Cupids. But he's confused about plurals. Can you help?

For each pair of underlined words, circle the correctly spelled plural noun.

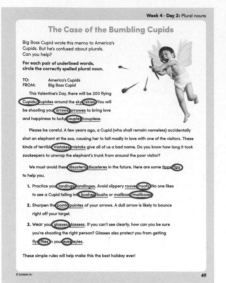

TO: America's Cupids
FROM: Big Boss Cupid

This Valentine's Day, there will be 200 flying (Cupids)/Cupides around the sky/(skies). You will be shooting your (arrows)/arrowes to bring love and happiness to lucky (couples)/coupleses.

Please be careful. A few years ago, a Cupid (who shall remain nameless) accidentally shot an elephant at the zoo, causing her to fall madly in love with one of the visitors. These kinds of terrible (mistakes)/mistaks give us all a bad name. Do you know how long it took zookeepers to unwrap the elephant's trunk from around the poor visitor?

We must avoid these (disasters)/disasteres in the future. Here are some (tipps)/tips to help you.

1. Practice your (landings)/landinges. Avoid slippery (roves)/(roofs). No one likes to see a Cupid falling into (bushes)/bushs or (mailboxs)/(mailboxes).

2. Sharpen the (points)/pointes of your arrows. A dull arrow is likely to bounce right off your target.

3. Wear your (glasses)/glasses. If you can't see clearly, how can you be sure you're shooting the right person? Glasses also protect you from getting (flys)/(flies) in your (eyes)/eyies.

These simple rules will help make this the best holiday ever!

49

Family Fun

Multiplication is the opposite of division. The product and factors can be used to write division sentences. The multiplication and division sentences are called a **fact family.**

2 x 6 = 12 (2 groups of 6)   12 ÷ 6 = 2 (12 divided into 6 equal groups)
6 x 2 = 12 (6 groups of 2)   12 ÷ 2 = 6 (12 divided into 2 equal groups)

Write two multiplication and two division sentences for each set of numbers.

1. 2, 3, 6
$$2 \times 3 = 6$$
$$3 \times 2 = 6$$
$$6 \div 2 = 3$$
$$6 \div 3 = 2$$

4. 3, 5, 15
$$3 \times 5 = 15$$
$$5 \times 3 = 15$$
$$15 \div 3 = 5$$
$$15 \div 5 = 3$$

7. 5, 6, 30
$$5 \times 6 = 30$$
$$6 \times 5 = 30$$
$$30 \div 5 = 6$$
$$30 \div 6 = 5$$

2. 2, 8, 16
$$2 \times 8 = 16$$
$$8 \times 2 = 16$$
$$16 \div 2 = 8$$
$$16 \div 8 = 2$$

5. 3, 9, 27
$$3 \times 9 = 27$$
$$9 \times 3 = 27$$
$$27 \div 3 = 9$$
$$27 \div 9 = 3$$

8. 6, 7, 42
$$6 \times 7 = 42$$
$$7 \times 6 = 42$$
$$42 \div 6 = 7$$
$$42 \div 7 = 6$$

3. 4, 5, 20
$$4 \times 5 = 20$$
$$5 \times 4 = 20$$
$$20 \div 4 = 5$$
$$20 \div 5 = 4$$

6. 5, 8, 40
$$8 \times 5 = 40$$
$$5 \times 8 = 40$$
$$40 \div 8 = 5$$
$$40 \div 5 = 8$$

9. 4, 8, 32
$$4 \times 8 = 32$$
$$8 \times 4 = 32$$
$$32 \div 4 = 8$$
$$32 \div 8 = 4$$

Challenge

Ramone has 33 marbles [...] each of 3 bags. How m[...] sheet of paper, write a [...] Then write the set of nu[...]

11 marbles
33÷3=11   33÷11=3
11x3=33   3x11=33

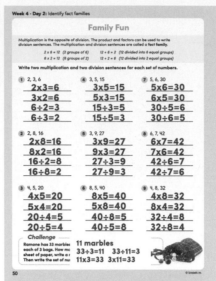

50

A Perfect Match?

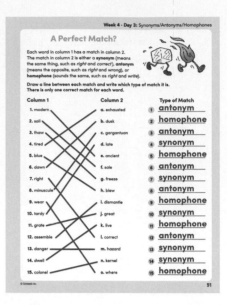

Each word in column 1 has a match in column 2. The match in column 2 is either a **synonym** (means the same thing, such as *right* and *correct*), **antonym** (means the opposite, such as *right* and *wrong*), or **homophone** (sounds the same, such as *right* and *write*).

Draw a line between each match and write which type of match it is. There is only one correct match for each word.

Column 1	Column 2	Type of Match
1. modern	a. exhausted	1. antonym
2. sail	b. dusk	2. homophone
3. thaw	c. gargantuan	3. antonym
4. tired	d. late	4. synonym
5. blue	e. ancient	5. homophone
6. dawn	f. sale	6. antonym
7. right	g. freeze	7. synonym
8. minuscule	h. blew	8. antonym
9. wear	i. dismantle	9. homophone
10. tardy	j. great	10. synonym
11. grate	k. live	11. homophone
12. assemble	l. correct	12. antonym
13. danger	m. hazard	13. synonym
14. dwell	n. kernel	14. synonym
15. colonel	o. where	15. homophone

51

Change It Up

The order of the factors in a multiplication sentence can change without changing the value of the product. If 2 x 7 is changed to 7 x 2, the product still equals 14.

Change the order of the factors in each multiplication sentence.

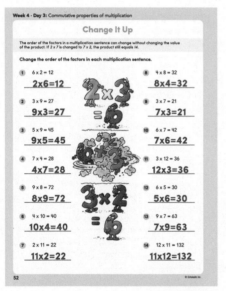

1. 6 x 2 = 12
$$2 \times 6 = 12$$

2. 3 x 9 = 27
$$9 \times 3 = 27$$

3. 5 x 9 = 45
$$9 \times 5 = 45$$

4. 7 x 4 = 28
$$4 \times 7 = 28$$

5. 9 x 8 = 72
$$8 \times 9 = 72$$

6. 4 x 10 = 40
$$10 \times 4 = 40$$

7. 2 x 11 = 22
$$11 \times 2 = 22$$

8. 4 x 8 = 32
$$8 \times 4 = 32$$

9. 3 x 7 = 21
$$7 \times 3 = 21$$

10. 6 x 7 = 42
$$7 \times 6 = 42$$

11. 3 x 12 = 36
$$12 \times 3 = 36$$

12. 6 x 5 = 30
$$5 \times 6 = 30$$

13. 9 x 7 = 63
$$7 \times 9 = 63$$

14. 12 x 11 = 132
$$11 \times 12 = 132$$

52

Glue Words

Conjunctions are words that join words or parts of sentences together. The most common conjunctions are *and*, *or*, and *but*. Each one means something different.

And joins words or phrases that go together equally.
Or gives you a choice.
But introduces something that contrasts with something earlier in the sentence.

Write *and*, *or*, or *but* on the blank lines where you think they belong.

1. I completely forgot to study for the big math test, **but** amazingly, I still got all the answers right.

2. He saved his money for a whole year, **and** he bought himself a new bicycle.

3. "Either clean up your room this minute," her mother said, "**or** you're not going to the movies tonight!"

4. The weather was beautiful, **and** everyone loved the parade.

5. Would you like Italian **or** Chinese food for dinner?

6. Her face was dirty, her clothes were torn, and she was far from the palace, **but** I immediately knew she was the princess.

7. He was selected "Student of the Year" because he got the highest grades, was elected class president, **and** raised the most money in the charity marathon.

8. I don't have much money left, so I can buy either a pizza **or** my favorite magazine, but not both.

9. I memorized the whole script before the audition and acted my heart and soul out for the director, **but** I still didn't get a part in the play.

10. I can't decide which dog to adopt from the animal rescue league: the pretty Pomeranian **or** the dashing Dalmatian.

53

Keep On Dividing

Use these steps when dividing larger numbers.

1. Divide the tens digit in the dividend by the divisor. Write the answer above the tens digit.
$$4\overline{)84}$$

2. Multiply the partial quotient by the divisor. Write the answer below the tens digit. Subtract. Bring down the ones digit.
$$\begin{array}{r} 2 \\ 4\overline{)84} \\ -8 \\ \hline 04 \end{array}$$

3. Divide the ones digit by the divisor. Write the answer above the ones digit. Multiply. Subtract.
$$\begin{array}{r} 21 \\ 4\overline{)84} \\ -8 \\ \hline 04 \\ -4 \\ \hline 0 \end{array}$$

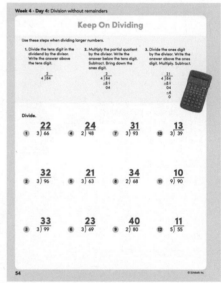

Divide.

1. $3\overline{)66} = 22$ 4. $2\overline{)48} = 24$ 7. $3\overline{)93} = 31$ 10. $3\overline{)39} = 13$

2. $3\overline{)96} = 32$ 5. $3\overline{)63} = 21$ 8. $2\overline{)68} = 34$ 11. $9\overline{)90} = 10$

3. $3\overline{)99} = 33$ 6. $3\overline{)69} = 23$ 9. $2\overline{)80} = 40$ 12. $5\overline{)55} = 11$

54

A Rainforest Find

Read the article. Then answer the questions on page 56.

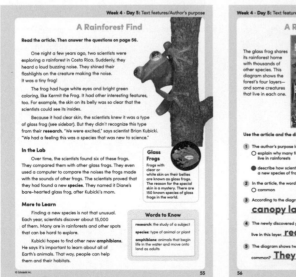

One night a few years ago, two scientists were exploring a rainforest in Costa Rica. Suddenly, they heard a loud buzzing noise. They shined their flashlights on the creature making the noise. It was a tiny frog!

The frog had huge white eyes and bright green coloring, like Kermit the Frog. It had other interesting features, too. For example, the skin on its belly was so clear that the scientists could see its insides.

Because it had clear skin, the scientists knew it was a type of glass frog (see sidebar). But they didn't recognize this type from their **research.** "We were excited," says scientist Brian Kubicki. "We had a feeling this was a species that was new to science."

In the Lab

Over time, the scientists found six of these frogs. They compared them with other glass frogs. They even used a computer to compare the noises the frogs made with the sounds of other frogs. The scientists proved that they had found a new **species.** They named it Diane's bare-hearted glass frog, after Kubicki's mom.

More to Learn

Finding a new species is not that unusual. Each year, scientists discover about 15,000 of them. Many are in rainforests and other spots that can be hard to explore.

Kubicki hopes to find other new **amphibians.** He says it's important to learn about all of Earth's animals. That way, people can help them and their habitats.

Glass Frogs

Frogs with clear or white skin on their bellies are known as glass frogs. The reason for the special skin is a mystery. There are 150 known species of glass frogs in the world.

Words to Know

research: the study of a subject

species: type of animal or plant

amphibians: animals that begin life in the water and move onto land as adults

55

A Rainforest Find (continued)

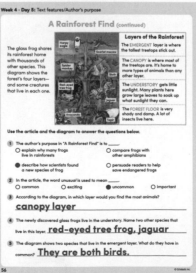

The glass frog shares its rainforest home with thousands of other species. This diagram shows the forest's four layers—and some creatures that live in each one.

Layers of the Rainforest

The EMERGENT layer is where the tallest treetops stick out.

The CANOPY is where most of the treetops are. It's home to more types of animals than any other layer.

The UNDERSTORY gets little sunlight. Many plants here grow large leaves to soak up what sunlight they can.

The FOREST FLOOR is very shady and damp. A lot of insects live here.

Use the article and the diagram to answer the questions below.

1. The author's purpose in "A Rainforest Find" is to __
   ○ explain why many frogs live in rainforests
   ○ compare frogs with other amphibians
   ● describe how scientists found a new species of frog
   ○ persuade readers to help save endangered frogs

2. In the article, the word *unusual* is used to mean __.
   ○ common   ○ exciting   ● uncommon   ○ important

3. According to the diagram, in which layer would you find the most animals?
   canopy layer

4. The newly discovered glass frogs live in the understory. Name two other species that live in this layer. **red-eyed tree frog, jaguar**

5. The diagram shows two species that live in the emergent layer. What do they have in common? **They are both birds.**

56

Week 5

134

Possessive Pronouns

Possessive pronouns come before nouns and show ownership.
Some possessive pronouns are: my, his, her, its, your, our, and their.
For example: Lisa has a pet frog. His name is Hopper.
His (possessive pronoun) takes the place of frog (noun).

Fill in the blanks with one of the possessive pronouns listed above.

1. The firemen showed __our__ class how to climb a ladder.
2. Peter cleaned __his__ room.
3. Kate loves to play soccer. __Her__ favorite position is goalie.
4. The students planned a surprise party for __their__ teacher.
5. "Mrs. Ruiz, please take __your__ students through the museum."
6. We celebrated __our__ team's win against the visitors.
7. "__My__ dog just had puppies," said Karen.
8. The boy thanked __his__ teacher for helping him with his French homework.
9. Bobby, Joel, and Jack helped __their__ coach put away the baseball equipment.
10. The spider spun __its__ web near the door.
11. Julie came into the room and asked, "Why are __your__ papers all over the floor?"
12. Why can't you put __your__ things away neatly?
13. After Vernon saw the movie, he got into __his__ car and drove away.
14. The girls said a few words and then put __their__ coats on and went home.
15. __Our__ mom was so tired that we cooked dinner for her.

59

Time for Math

Fill in the circle for each correct answer.

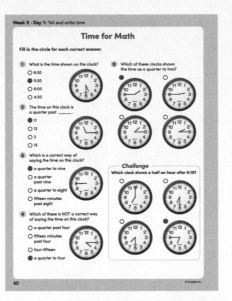

1. What is the time shown on the clock?
   - 6:30
   - **5:30**
   - 6:00
   - 4:30

2. The time on this clock is a quarter past _____.
   - **11**
   - 12
   - 3
   - 15

3. Which is a correct way of saying the time on this clock?
   - **a quarter to nine**
   - a quarter past nine
   - a quarter to eight
   - fifteen minutes past eight

4. Which of these is NOT a correct way of saying the time on this clock?
   - a quarter past four
   - fifteen minutes past four
   - four-fifteen
   - **a quarter to four**

5. Which of these clocks shows the time as a quarter to two?

Challenge
Which clock shows a half an hour after 6:15?

60

Colorful Clues

You can compare two things that are not alike in order to give your readers a clearer and more colorful picture. When you use like or as to make a comparison, it is called a simile.
Max is as slow as molasses when he doesn't want to do something.
My sister leaped over the puddles like a frog to avoid getting her shoes wet.
The angry man erupted like a volcano.

When you make a comparison without like or as, it is called a metaphor. You compare things directly, saying the subject is something else.
The disturbed anthill was a whirlwind of activity.
The oak trees, silent sentries around the cabin, stood guard.
Jenny and I were all ears as we listened to the latest gossip.

Finish the metaphors and similes. **Answers will vary.**

1. Crowds of commuters piled into the subway cars like _____
_____

2. Chirping crickets on a warm summer night are _____

3. After rolling in the mud, our dog looked like _____

4. Happiness is _____

5. Just learning to walk, the toddler was as wobbly as _____

6. After scoring the winning point, I felt as _____

7. Having a tooth filled is about as much fun as _____

8. _____ is like _____

61

Working With Area

The area of an object is the number of square units needed to cover its surface. To find the area, multiply the length by the width.

4 x 2 = 8 square units

Write a number sentence to find the area of each shape. Then, on another sheet of paper, write the multiplication and division fact family for each number sentence.

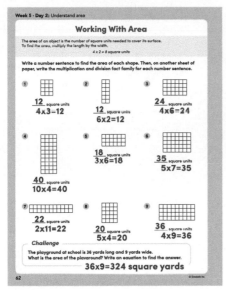

1. __12__ square units
4x3=12

2. __12__ square units
6x2=12

3. __24__ square units
4x6=24

4. __18__ square units
3x6=18

5. __35__ square units
5x7=35

6. __40__ square units
10x4=40

7. __22__ square units
2x11=22

8. __20__ square units
5x4=20

9. __36__ square units
4x9=36

Challenge
The playground at school is 36 yards long and 9 yards wide. What is the area of the playground? Write an equation to find the answer.
__36x9=324 square yards__

62

Where's the Action?

A verb tells the action in a sentence.

Fill in the bubble beneath the word that is a verb.

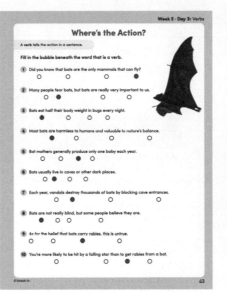

1. Did you know that bats are the only mammals that can fly?
2. Many people fear bats, but bats are really very important to us.
3. Bats eat half their body weight in bugs every night.
4. Most bats are harmless to humans and valuable to nature's balance.
5. Bat mothers generally produce only one baby each year.
6. Bats usually live in caves or other dark places.
7. Each year, vandals destroy thousands of bats by blocking cave entrances.
8. Bats are not really blind, but some people believe they are.
9. As for the belief that bats carry rabies, this is untrue.
10. You're more likely to be hit by a falling star than to get rabies from a bat.

63

How Many Square Units?

Shade in a shape that matches the given area. The first one is done for you.

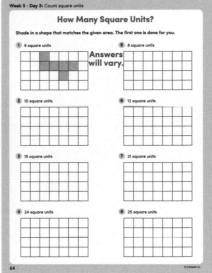

1. 6 square units   **Answers will vary.**
2. 10 square units
3. 15 square units
4. 24 square units
5. 8 square units
6. 12 square units
7. 21 square units
8. 25 square units

64

Let's Eat Out!

Two sentences can be combined to make one sentence by using the words: although, after, because, until, and while.

Choose a word from the menu to combine the two sentences into one sentence.

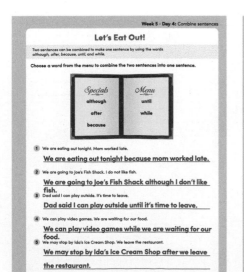

Specials
although
after
because

Menu
until
while

1. We are eating out tonight. Mom worked late.
We are eating out tonight because mom worked late.

2. We are going to Joe's Fish Shack. I do not like fish.
We are going to Joe's Fish Shack although I don't like fish.

3. Dad said I can play outside. It's time to leave.
Dad said I can play outside until it's time to leave.

4. We can play video games. We are waiting for our food.
We can play video games while we are waiting for our food.

5. We may stop by Ida's Ice Cream Shop. We leave the restaurant.
We may stop by Ida's Ice Cream Shop after we leave the restaurant.

65

Picture Perfect

An array shows a multiplication sentence. The first factor tells how many rows there are. The second factor tells how many are in each row. Here is an array for the multiplication sentence 4 x 4 = 16.

4 rows
x 4 rows
16 in all

Solve each problem by creating an array.

1. 3 x 4 = **12**
2. 2 x 5 = **10**
3. 8 x 5 = **40**
4. 6 x 5 = **30**
5. 6 x 4 = **24**
6. 3 x 5 = **15**

66

Kadimba's Field
Bantu Folktale

How does Kadimba use his cleverness to avoid work?

1 Clever Kadimba was a lazy hare. It was time to plant crops to feed
2 his family, but he hated work. Tangled bushes throughout his field
3 made the job daunting. Even after clearing the field, Kadimba would
4 still have to dig rows for his crops.
5 Kadimba hatched a plan. He dragged a thick rope across his field.
6 Then he waited by one end for Elephant to appear. Kadimba dared
7 Elephant to a tug-of-war. Elephant roared but agreed. He twisted
8 his trunk around the rope. Kadimba said, "When you feel my pull,
9 then pull back." He raced to the opposite side of the tangled field
10 and rested by the other end of the rope. Elephant waited patiently.
11 Soon Hippo waddled by. Kadimba offered this giant the same
12 challenge. Hippo agreed, letting the hare wrap the rope around his
13 muddy body. Kadimba said, "When you feel my pull, then pull
14 back." Hippo waited good-naturedly.
15 Kadimba then dashed to the middle of the rope and tugged in
16 each direction. Feeling the pull, Elephant and Hippo began tugging.
17 They yanked, grunted, and
18 heaved in astonishment.
19 They pulled back and forth,
20 left and right, struggling
21 until nightfall. By then, the
22 rope had torn out all
23 the tangled bushes;
24 the thrashing had softened the
25 soil. Kadimba's field was
26 ready for planting.

67

135

Kadimba's Field (continued)

Answer each question. Give evidence from the folktale.

Possible answers shown.

1. The **daunting** job (line 3) made Kadimba feel _____.
   ○ heartbroken   ● discouraged   ○ sleepy   ○ proud
   How did you choose your answer? __Kadimba was lazy and hated__
   __work (lines 1–2). He didn't look forward to the huge job.__

2. Which type of character is Kadimba? _____.
   ○ a brave hero   ● a sneaky trickster
   ○ an angry loser   ○ an innocent victim
   What in the text helped you answer? __Kadimba fooled Elephant and__
   __Hippo into thinking they were going to have a tug-of-war__
   __with him but really he wanted them to clear his field for__
   __planting (lines 5–7, 11–13, 15–26).__

3. Why did Hippo and Elephant feel so astonished (lines 17–18)? __Each one expected__
   __the tug-of-war against the small hare to end quickly__
   __with himself as an easy winner (lines 7–14).__

4. Why did Kadimba rest for a while (lines 9–11)? __He had to wait for another__
   __strong animal to come along and play (lines 11–13).__

5. Explain Kadimba's clever plan. __Clearing the field was hard for a__
   __hare, but easy for big strong animals. He tricked__
   __Elephant and Hippo into clearing his field by tricking__
   __them into a tug-of-war (lines 5–7, 11–12, 15–26).__

68

Week 6

The Apology of Goldilocks

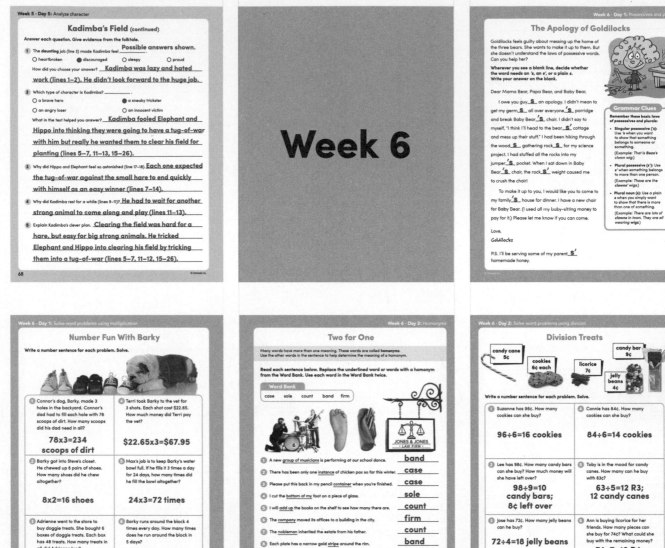

Goldilocks feels guilty about messing up the home of the three bears. She wants to make it up to them. But she doesn't understand the laws of possessive words. Can you help her?

Wherever you see a blank line, decide whether the word needs an 's, an s', or a plain s. Write your answer on the blank.

Dear Mama Bear, Papa Bear, and Baby Bear,

   I owe you guy**_s_** an apology. I didn't mean to get my germ**_s_** all over everyone**_'s_** porridge and break Baby Bear**_'s_** chair. I didn't say to myself, "I think I'll head to the bear**_s'_** cottage and mess up their stuff." I had been hiking through the wood**_s_** gathering rock**_s_** for my science project. I had stuffed all the rocks into my jumper**_'s_** pocket. When I sat down in Baby Bear**_'s_** chair, the rock**_s'_** weight caused me to crush the chair!

   To make it up to you, I would like you to come to my family**_'s_** house for dinner. I have a new chair for Baby Bear. (I used all my baby-sitting money to pay for it.) Please let me know if you can come.

Love,
Goldilocks

P.S. I'll be serving some of my parent**_s'_** homemade honey.

Grammar Clues

Remember these basic laws of possessives and plurals:

- **Singular possessive ('s):** Use 's when you want to show that something belongs to someone or something.
  (Example: *That is Bozo's clown wig.*)

- **Plural possessive (s'):** Use s' when something belongs to more than one person.
  (Example: *Those are the clowns' wigs.*)

- **Plural noun (s):** Use a plain s when you simply want to show that there is more than one of something.
  (Example: *There are lots of clowns in town. They are all wearing wigs.*)

71

Number Fun With Barky

Write a number sentence for each problem. Solve.

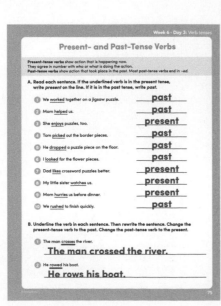

1. Connor's dog, Barky, made 3 holes in the backyard. Connor's dad had to fill each hole with 78 scoops of dirt. How many scoops did his dad need in all?
   78x3=234 scoops of dirt

2. Barky got into Steve's closet. He chewed up 8 pairs of shoes. How many shoes did he chew altogether?
   8x2=16 shoes

3. Adrienne went to the store to buy doggie treats. She bought 6 boxes of doggie treats. Each box has 48 treats. How many treats in all did Adrienne buy?
   48x6=288 treats

4. Terri took Barky to the vet for 3 shots. Each shot cost $22.65. How much money did Terri pay the vet?
   $22.65x3=$67.95

5. Max's job is to keep Barky's water bowl full. If he fills it 3 times a day for 24 days, how many times did he fill the bowl altogether?
   24x3=72 times

6. Barky runs around the block 4 times every day. How many times does he run around the block in 5 days?
   4x5=20 times

72

Two for One

Many words have more than one meaning. These words are called **homonyms**.
Use the other words in the sentence to help determine the meaning of a homonym.

Read each sentence below. Replace the underlined word or words with a homonym from the Word Bank. Use each word in the Word Bank twice.

Word Bank

case   sole   count   band   firm

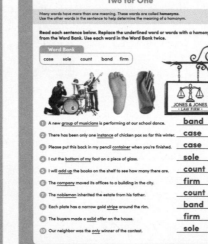

JONES & JONES LAW FIRM

1. A new <u>group</u> of musicians is performing at our school dance.   **band**
2. There has been only one <u>instance</u> of chicken pox so far this winter.   **case**
3. Please put this back in my pencil <u>container</u> when you're finished.   **case**
4. I cut the <u>bottom</u> of my foot on a piece of glass.   **sole**
5. I will <u>add up</u> the books on the shelf to see how many there are.   **count**
6. The <u>company</u> moved its offices to a building in the city.   **firm**
7. The <u>nobleman</u> inherited the estate from his father.   **count**
8. Each plate has a narrow gold <u>stripe</u> around the rim.   **band**
9. The buyers made a <u>solid</u> offer on the house.   **firm**
10. Our neighbor was the <u>only</u> winner of the contest.   **sole**

73

Division Treats

candy cane 5¢
cookies 6¢ each
licorice 7¢
candy bar 9¢
jelly beans 4¢

Write a number sentence for each problem. Solve.

1. Suzanne has 96¢. How many cookies can she buy?
   96÷6=16 cookies

2. Lee has 98¢. How many candy bars can she buy? How much money will she have left over?
   98÷9=10 candy bars; 8¢ left over

3. Jose has 72¢. How many jelly beans can he buy?
   72÷4=18 jelly beans

4. Connie has 84¢. How many cookies can she buy?
   84÷6=14 cookies

5. Toby is in the mood for candy canes. How many can he buy with 63¢?
   63÷5=12 R3; 12 candy canes

6. Ann is buying licorice for her friends. How many pieces can she buy with the remaining money?
   74÷7=10 R4; 10 pieces of licorice; a jelly bean for 4¢

74

Present- and Past-Tense Verbs

Present-tense verbs show action that is happening now. They agree in number with who or what is doing the action.
Past-tense verbs show action that took place in the past. Most past-tense verbs end in -ed.

A. Read each sentence. If the underlined verb is in the present tense, write *present* on the line. If it is in the past tense, write *past*.

1. We <u>worked</u> together on a jigsaw puzzle.   **past**
2. Mom <u>helped</u> us.   **past**
3. She <u>enjoys</u> puzzles, too.   **present**
4. Tom <u>picked</u> out the border pieces.   **past**
5. He <u>dropped</u> a puzzle piece on the floor.   **past**
6. I <u>looked</u> for the flower pieces.   **past**
7. Dad <u>likes</u> crossword puzzles better.   **present**
8. My little sister <u>watches</u> us.   **present**
9. Mom <u>hurries</u> us before dinner.   **present**
10. We <u>rushed</u> to finish quickly.   **past**

B. Underline the verb in each sentence. Then rewrite the sentence. Change the present-tense verb to the past. Change the past-tense verb to the present.

1. The man <u>crosses</u> the river.
   The man crossed the river.

2. He <u>rowed</u> his boat.
   He rows his boat.

75

Multiply the Groups

Write the number of groups and the number of objects in each group. Then write a complete multiplication fact that relates to each picture. The first one is done for you.

1. __3 groups of 8__
   __3 x 8 = 24__

2. __4 groups of 9__
   __4x9=36__

3. __6 groups of 4__
   __6x4=24__

4. __4 groups of 5__
   __4x5=20__

5. __7 groups of 3__
   __7x3=21__

6. __9 groups of 2__
   __9x2=18__

76

That Drives Me Crazy!

The sentences that follow the topic sentence tell more about the topic. They are called **supporting sentences**.

Read the paragraph below. Cross out the three sentences that do not support the topic.

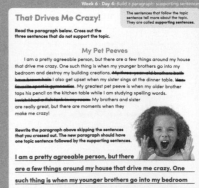

My Pet Peeves

   I am a pretty agreeable person, but there are a few things around my house that drive me crazy. One such thing is when my younger brothers go into my bedroom and destroy my building creations. ~~My three-year-old brothers both have brown hair.~~ I also get upset when my sister sings at the dinner table. ~~Her favorite sport is gymnastics.~~ My greatest pet peeve is when my older brother taps his pencil on the kitchen table while I am studying spelling words. ~~I wish I had a fish tank in my room.~~ My brothers and sister are really great, but there are moments when they make me crazy!

Rewrite the paragraph above skipping the sentences that you crossed out. The new paragraph should have one topic sentence followed by the supporting sentences.

I am a pretty agreeable person, but there are a few things around my house that drive me crazy. One such thing is when my younger brothers go into my bedroom and destroy my building creations. I also get upset when my sister sings at the dinner table. My greatest pet peeve is when my older brother taps his pencil on the kitchen table while I am studying spelling words. My brothers and sister are really great, but there are moments when they make me crazy!

77

Find the Product

Write the product of each statement.

x	1	2	3	4	5	6	7	8	9	10
1	1	2	3	4	5	6	7	8	9	10
2	2	4	6	8	10	12	14	16	18	20
3	3	6	9	12	15	18	21	24	27	30
4	4	8	12	16	20	24	28	32	36	40
5	5	10	15	20	25	30	35	40	45	50
6	6	12	18	24	30	36	42	48	54	60
7	7	14	21	28	35	42	49	56	63	70
8	8	16	24	32	40	48	56	64	72	80
9	9	18	27	36	45	54	63	72	81	90
10	10	20	30	40	50	60	70	80	90	100

1 7 × 30 = __210__   6 6 × 20 = __120__   11 50 × 9 = __450__

2 40 × 7 = __280__   7 60 × 8 = __480__   12 80 × 3 = __240__

3 50 × 50 = __2,500__   8 20 × 90 = __1,800__   13 50 × 90 = __4,500__

4 9 × 500 = __4,500__   9 300 × 30 = __9,000__   14 70 × 100 = __7,000__

5 20 × 600 = __12,000__   10 9,000 × 7 = __63,000__   15 400 × 20 = __8,000__

78

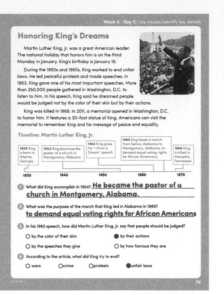

Honoring King's Dreams

Martin Luther King, Jr. was a great American leader. The national holiday that honors him is on the third Monday in January. King's birthday is January 15.

During the 1950s and 1960s, King worked to end unfair laws. He led peaceful protests and made speeches. In 1963, King gave one of his most important speeches. More than 250,000 people gathered in Washington, D.C. to listen to him. In his speech, King said he dreamed people would be judged not by the color of their skin but by their actions.

King was killed in 1968. In 2011, a memorial opened in Washington, D.C. to honor him. It features a 30-foot statue of King. Americans can visit the memorial to remember King and his message of peace and equality.

Timeline: Martin Luther King, Jr.

1929 King is born in Atlanta, Georgia — 1954 King becomes the pastor of a church in Montgomery, Alabama — 1963 King gives his "I Have a Dream" speech — 1965 King leads a march from Selma, Alabama to Montgomery, Alabama, to demand equal voting rights for African Americans — 1968 King is killed in Memphis, Tennessee

1930   1940   1950   1960   1970

1 What did King accomplish in 1954? __He became the pastor of a church in Montgomery, Alabama.__

2 What was the purpose of the march that King led in Alabama in 1965? __to demand equal voting rights for African Americans__

3 In his 1963 speech, how did Martin Luther King, Jr. say that people should be judged?
○ by the color of their skin   ● by their actions
○ by the speeches they give   ○ by how famous they are

4 According to the article, what did King try to end?
○ wars   ○ crime   ○ protests   ● unfair laws

79

Incentive Chart: Week 1

Week 1	Day 1	Day 2	Day 3	Day 4	Day 5
Put a sticker to show you completed each day's work.	☆	☆	☆	☆	☆
	☆	☆	☆	☆	☆

CONGRATULATIONS!

Wow! You did a great job this week!

This certificate is presented to:

_____

Date   Parent/Caregiver's Signature

Week 7

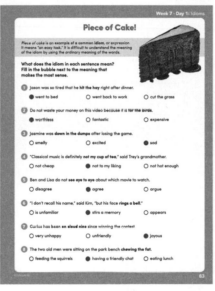

Piece of Cake!

Piece of cake is an example of a common idiom, or expression. It means "an easy task." It is difficult to understand the meaning of the idiom by using the ordinary meaning of the words.

What does the idiom in each sentence mean? Fill in the bubble next to the meaning that makes the most sense.

1 Jason was so tired that he **hit the hay** right after dinner.
● went to bed   ○ went back to work   ○ cut the grass

2 Do not waste your money on this video because it is **for the birds.**
● worthless   ○ fantastic   ○ expensive

3 Jasmine was **down in the dumps** after losing the game.
○ smelly   ○ excited   ● sad

4 "Classical music is definitely **not my cup of tea**," said Trey's grandmother.
○ not cheap   ● not to my liking   ○ not hot enough

5 Ben and Lisa do not **see eye to eye** about which movie to watch.
● disagree   ○ agree   ○ argue

6 "I don't recall his name," said Kim, "but his face **rings a bell.**"
○ is unfamiliar   ● stirs a memory   ○ appears

7 Carlos has been **on cloud nine** since winning the contest.
○ very unhappy   ○ unfriendly   ● joyous

8 The two old men were sitting on the park bench **chewing the fat.**
○ feeding the squirrels   ● having a friendly chat   ○ eating lunch

83

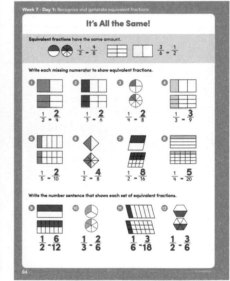

It's All the Same!

Equivalent fractions have the same amount.

$\frac{1}{2} = \frac{4}{8}$ $\frac{3}{6} = \frac{1}{2}$

Write each missing numerator to show equivalent fractions.

1 $\frac{1}{2} = \frac{2}{4}$ 2 $\frac{1}{3} = \frac{2}{6}$ 3 $\frac{1}{4} = \frac{2}{8}$ 4 $\frac{1}{3} = \frac{3}{9}$

5 $\frac{1}{5} = \frac{2}{10}$ 6 $\frac{1}{4} = \frac{2}{8}$ 7 $\frac{1}{2} = \frac{8}{16}$ 8 $\frac{1}{4} = \frac{5}{20}$

Write the number sentence that shows each set of equivalent fractions.

9 $\frac{1}{2} = \frac{6}{12}$ 10 $\frac{1}{3} = \frac{2}{6}$ 11 $\frac{1}{3} = \frac{6}{18}$ 12 $\frac{1}{2} = \frac{3}{6}$

84

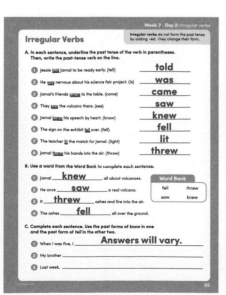

Irregular Verbs

Irregular verbs do not form the past tense by adding *-ed*. They change their form.

A. In each sentence, underline the past tense of the verb in parentheses. Then, write the past-tense verb on the line.

1 Jessie <u>told</u> Jamal to be ready early. (tell) __told__

2 He <u>was</u> nervous about his science fair project. (is) __was__

3 Jamal's friends <u>came</u> to the table. (come) __came__

4 They <u>saw</u> the volcano there. (see) __saw__

5 Jamal <u>knew</u> his speech by heart. (know) __knew__

6 The sign on the exhibit <u>fell</u> over. (fall) __fell__

7 The teacher <u>lit</u> the match for Jamal. (light) __lit__

8 Jamal <u>threw</u> his hands into the air. (throw) __threw__

B. Use a word from the Word Bank to complete each sentence.

1 Jamal __knew__ all about volcanoes.

2 He once __saw__ a real volcano.

3 It __threw__ ashes and fire into the air.

4 The ashes __fell__ all over the ground.

Word Bank
fell   threw
saw   knew

C. Complete each sentence. Use the past forms of *know* in one and the past form of *fell* in the other two.

__Answers will vary.__

1 When I was five, I _____

2 My brother _____

3 Last week, _____

85

Creature Count

A **pictograph** uses symbols to represent data. Use the chart on the right and the information in the problems below to make a pictograph.

Number of Select Animals at London Zoo, January 2012	
Blue Spiny Lizard	25
Moon Jellyfish	90
Short-Tailed Bat	200
Naked Mole Rat	35
Rasbora (fish)	65

1 Label the rows in the vertical axis of your graph with the name of each animal. What should you label the horizontal axis? __Number of Animals__

2 Decide on an icon for your pictograph. Each icon will represent the same number of animals. The icon should be easy to draw, and you should also be able to draw half of one. Draw your icon in the box.

Icons will vary.

3 Decide how many animals will be represented by each icon. Which number will allow you to best represent your data? ○ 5   ● 10   ○ 100

4 Draw your graph below. Make sure it has a title, labels, and icons based on the data in the chart. Add a key that explains how many animals each icon represents.

Title: __Titles will vary__

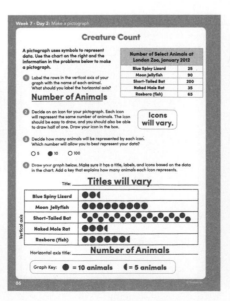

Blue Spiny Lizard	●●◖
Moon Jellyfish	●●●●●●●●●
Short-Tailed Bat	●●●●●●●●●●●●●●●●●●●●
Naked Mole Rat	●●●◖
Rasbora (fish)	●●●●●●◖

Horizontal axis title: __Number of Animals__

Graph Key: ● = 10 animals   ◖ = 5 animals

86

Suffixes

A **suffix** is a word part that is added to the end of a word. A suffix changes the meaning of a word.

-ness and *-ment* mean "a state of being"   *-ly* means "in that way"
-ful means "full of"   *-er* means "a person who acts as"

A. Underline the suffix in each word below. Write the number of the word next to its definition on the right.

1 dark<u>ness</u>   __4__ to do something in a quick way
2 govern<u>ment</u>   __5__ a person who works on a ranch
3 grace<u>ful</u>   __2__ a group that governs a city, state or nation
4 rapid<u>ly</u>   __3__ moving in a smooth way, full of grace
5 ranch<u>er</u>   __1__ the state of being dark

B. Add a suffix to each word to form a new word. Use the meaning in parentheses to help you.

1 eager __ness__ (state of being)   4 paint __er__ (one who does something)

2 catch __er__ (one who does something)   5 distant __ly__ (in that way)

3 plenti __ful__ (full of)   6 amaze __ment__ (state of being)

C. Read the words. Write a word that means almost the same thing.

1 fast, speedily, quickly __rapidly__
2 surprise, astonishment, shock __amazement__
3 much, lots, boundless __plentiful__
4 beautiful, elegant, charming __graceful__

87

Figure It Out

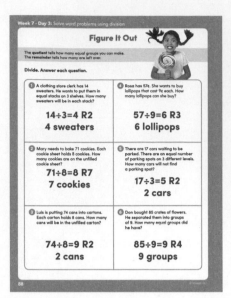

The **quotient** tells how many equal groups you can make.
The **remainder** tells how many are left over.

Divide. Answer each question.

① A clothing store clerk has 14 sweaters. He wants to put them in equal stacks on 3 shelves. How many sweaters will be in each stack?

$14 \div 3 = 4$ R2
4 sweaters

④ Rosa has 57¢. She wants to buy lollipops that cost 9¢ each. How many lollipops can she buy?

$57 \div 9 = 6$ R3
6 lollipops

② Mary needs to bake 71 cookies. Each cookie sheet holds 8 cookies. How many cookies are on the unfilled cookie sheet?

$71 \div 8 = 8$ R7
7 cookies

⑤ There are 17 cars waiting to be parked. There are an equal number of parking spots on 3 different levels. How many cars will not find a parking spot?

$17 \div 3 = 5$ R2
2 cars

③ Luis is putting 74 cans into cartons. Each carton holds 8 cans. How many cans will be in the unfilled carton?

$74 \div 8 = 9$ R2
2 cans

⑥ Don bought 85 crates of flowers. He separated them into groups of 9. How many equal groups did he have?

$85 \div 9 = 9$ R4
9 groups

88

Where Are We Going?

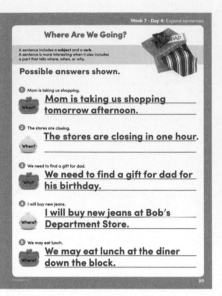

A sentence includes a **subject** and a **verb**.
A sentence is more interesting when it also includes a part that tells where, when, or why.

Possible answers shown.

① Mom is taking us shopping.
When?
Mom is taking us shopping tomorrow afternoon.

② The stores are closing.
When?
The stores are closing in one hour.

③ We need to find a gift for dad.
Why?
We need to find a gift for dad for his birthday.

④ I will buy new jeans.
Where?
I will buy new jeans at Bob's Department Store.

⑤ We may eat lunch.
Where?
We may eat lunch at the diner down the block.

89

Calculating Area

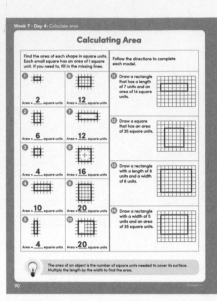

Find the area of each shape in square units. Each small square has an area of 1 square unit. If you need to, fill in the missing lines.

Follow the directions to complete each model.

① Area = __2__ square units

⑥ Area = __12__ square units

⑪ Draw a rectangle that has a length of 7 units and an area of 14 square units.

② Area = __6__ square units

⑦ Area = __12__ square units

⑫ Draw a square that has an area of 25 square units.

③ Area = __4__ square units

⑧ Area = __16__ square units

⑬ Draw a rectangle with a length of 8 units and a width of 6 units.

④ Area = __10__ square units

⑨ Area = __20__ square units

⑭ Draw a rectangle with a width of 5 units and an area of 35 square units.

⑤ Area = __4__ square units

⑩ Area = __20__ square units

💡 The area of an object is the number of square units needed to cover its surface. Multiply the length by the width to find the area.

90

Follow Me

What makes this story an adventure?

1 "When this volcano blew about a thousand years ago,
2 it sent the local inhabitants scurrying to safety," Mimi
3 reported as we neared our destination.
4   We drove through a moonlike landscape, where plants
5 and trees struggled to grow. Then I saw Sunset Crater. It
6 was a huge black cone with tinges of orange and yellow.
7 It was magnificent! We parked the car and began to walk
8 the winding trail along its base. "I've got the flashlights,"
9 Mimi said.
10   Flashlights? I wondered. I soon found out the
11 reason for them when she
12 stopped and pointed to a
13 narrow, dark opening. "Follow
14 me," she called. "We're about
15 to enter a tunnel made by
16 lava. Zip up your sweatshirt."
17   We scrambled down into
18 darkness. It got cold very
19 quickly as we descended; it
20 got scary, too. We clambered
21 over sharp and slippery rocks and had to duck under
22 hanging rocks that looked like icicles. The ceiling was so
23 low in parts that we had to crawl. Soon the walls began to
24 close in on us. At that point we stopped, took in the eerie
25 silence, and then made our way out.
26   "Amazing lava tube, right?" Mimi asked, once we were
27 safely above ground.
28   "Awesome!" I answered, relieved to see blue sky.

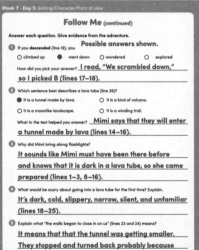

91

Follow Me (continued)

Answer each question. Give evidence from the adventure.

Possible answers shown.

① If you **descended** (line 19), you
○ climbed up   ● went down   ○ wondered   ○ explored

How did you pick your answer? __I read, "We scrambled down,"__
__so I picked B (lines 17–18).__

② Which sentence best describes a lava tube (line 26)?
● It is a tunnel made by lava.   ○ It is a kind of volcano.
○ It is a moonlike landscape.   ○ It is a winding trail.

What in the text helped you answer? __Mimi says that they will enter__
__a tunnel made by lava (lines 14–16).__

③ Why did Mimi bring along flashlights?
__It sounds like Mimi must have been there before__
__and knows that it is dark in a lava tube, so she came__
__prepared (lines 1–3, 8–16).__

④ What would be scary about going into a lava tube for the first time? Explain.
__It's dark, cold, slippery, narrow, silent, and unfamiliar__
__(lines 18–25).__

⑤ Explain what "the walls began to close in on us" (lines 23 and 24) means?
__It means that that the tunnel was getting smaller.__
__They stopped and turned back probably because__
__there wasn't room to go farther (lines 22–25).__

92

Week 8

Describe the Action

Adverbs can tell when, where, how, or how much.

Most deserts in the United States are very hot and dry. Plants and animals have adapted to live in deserts. For example, many plants have far-reaching roots to search for water. Some cacti swell up to store water. Animals have also developed varied ways of dealing with the heat and lack of water.

Use what you know to draw conclusions about desert plants and animals. Answer the questions below using one or more of the adverbs from the Word Bank. Complete the sentences.

Possible answers shown.

Word Bank

| always | eagerly | loudly | rarely |
| slowly | occasionally | usually | very |

① When does it rain in the desert?
It __rarely__ rains in the desert.

② How do most animals move in the heat?
Most animals move __slowly or occasionally__

③ How does a cactus grow?
A cactus grows __slowly__

④ How do thirsty creatures drink?
Thirsty creatures drink __eagerly__

⑤ How often should you drink water when you are in the desert?
When I am in the desert, I should __always drink water__

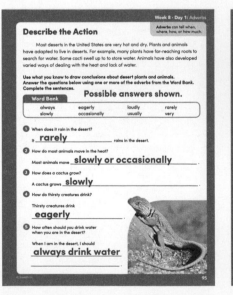

95

Over the Hurdles

Sometimes when you try to divide a number into equal groups, part of the number is left over. This is called the **remainder.** Use these steps to find the remainder.

$$5 \overline{)16}$$

$$\begin{array}{r} 3 \\ 5\overline{)16} \\ -15 \\ \hline 1 \end{array}$$

$$\begin{array}{r} 3\ R1 \\ 5\overline{)16} \\ -15 \\ \hline 1 \end{array}$$

Think: $5 \times$ ___ is the closest to 16?

There are 5 groups of 3 with 1 left over.

Divide.

①
$6\overline{)10}$ = 1 R4
$2\overline{)9}$ = 4 R1

②
$3\overline{)20}$ = 6 R2
$2\overline{)19}$ = 9 R1
$6\overline{)47}$ = 7 R5
$6\overline{)41}$ = 6 R5

③
$7\overline{)51}$ = 7 R2
$2\overline{)15}$ = 7 R1
$3\overline{)22}$ = 7 R1
$7\overline{)48}$ = 6 R6

④
$2\overline{)11}$ = 5 R1
$4\overline{)26}$ = 6 R2
$6\overline{)19}$ = 3 R1
$5\overline{)27}$ = 5 R2

96

Which One Do You Mean?

Homographs are words that have the same spellings but different meanings and pronunciations. For example, when you refer to a female hog, *sow* rhymes with *cow.* When you scatter seeds, *sow* rhymes with *no.*

Say both pronunciations for each homograph. Then write the letter for the correct pronunciation for the homographs in the sentences. Use a dictionary if you are not sure of the meaning of a word.

refuse	a. (ref-yoos)	minute	a. (min-it)	close	a. (klohs)
	b. (ri-fyooz)		b. (mye-noot)		b. (klohss)
wound	a. (wound)	object	a. (ob-jikt)	bow	a. (bou)
	b. (woond)		b. (uhb-jekt)		b. (boh)

① Give me a **minute** __a__ to adjust the microscope, so you can clearly see the **minute** __b__ germs.

② The doctor cleaned the **wound** __b__ on my arm and then **wound** __a__ a bandage around it.

③ I **refuse** __b__ to carry the **refuse** __a__ to the dumpster unless it is all in a sealed plastic bag.

④ Please **close** __a__ the window that is **close** __b__ to my desk.

⑤ The **bow** __b__ in my hair fell out as I gave a **bow** __a__ after my recital.

⑥ Would you **object** __b__ if I put this **object** __a__ on your desk?

97

Plot It!

Create a line plot based on the given numbers.

1. 1, 4, 5, 4, 7, 5, 4, 3, 5

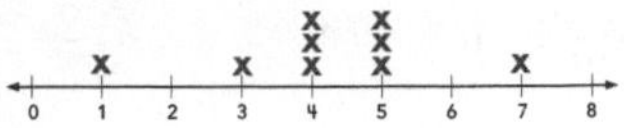

2. 4, $5\frac{1}{2}$, 6, $5\frac{1}{2}$, $3\frac{1}{2}$, $3\frac{1}{2}$, 5, $5\frac{1}{2}$, 5

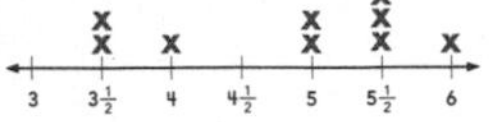

3. $8\frac{1}{2}$, $9\frac{1}{2}$, 9, 8, $7\frac{1}{2}$, $7\frac{1}{2}$, $7\frac{1}{2}$, $9\frac{1}{2}$, $7\frac{1}{2}$

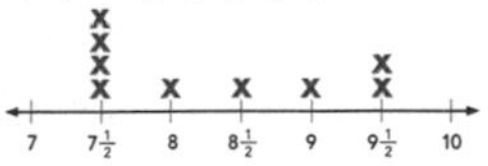

4. $5\frac{3}{4}$, $6\frac{1}{4}$, $5\frac{3}{4}$, 7, $6\frac{1}{4}$, $6\frac{1}{2}$, $6\frac{3}{4}$, $5\frac{3}{4}$, 7

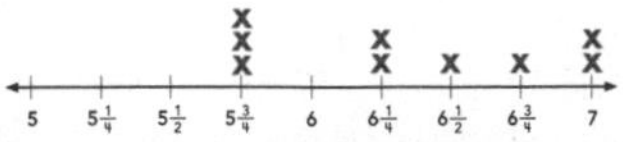

The Case of the Unexpected Delay

Will the Gingerbread Man's delicious new house ever be completed? Not if the hungry workers can help it!

Circle all the adjectives and underline all the adverbs in the letter below.

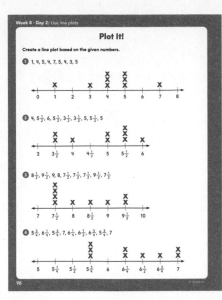

Dear Mr. Gingerbread Man,

We have some (bad) news. The (big) additions you asked us to build on your (gingerbread) house haven't been going as originally planned. Something (strange) is happening. Please let me humbly explain.

You must know that (coconut) lollipops, (sticky) toffee bars, and (giant) candy canes are not (normal) materials for building a (new) bedroom. But when I asked my (loyal) employees, they said that they would joyfully welcome the (unusual) challenge. (Big) Tony was especially (excited). He even started anxiously licking his lips.

On the (first) day of work, I noticed that we were using up (purple) gumdrops faster than I'd expected. And the order I had placed for (giant) jawbreakers was (short) by nearly a hundred. Then the (huge) crate of (red) licorice we were using for the (inside) walls disappeared!

Suddenly my (favorite) workers are regularly calling in (sick). (Heavy) Hank told me he had (seventeen) cavities. He's going to be out for a week getting them professionally drilled. (Chubby) Chuck has gotten so chubby that he fell through the (graham-cracker) roof. I don't know what's happening to them. Maybe they need more (physical) exercise.

Please, just give us (more) time. We'll quickly do a (wonderful) job.

Sincerely,

Do-It-All Builders, Inc.

Grammar Clues

- An **adjective** describes a noun or a pronoun. It might tell what kind, which one, or how many. (Example: *My two best friends gave me the most wonderful surprise ever!*)
- An **adverb** describes a verb, an adjective, or another adverb. Many adverbs end in *-ly*. (Example: *I quickly finished my homework so I could watch TV.*)

Comparing Fractions

Each pair of fractions has the same denominator. Compare each pair of fractions. Use the symbols <, >, or =.

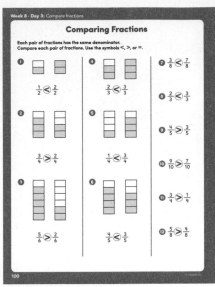

1. $\frac{1}{2} < \frac{2}{2}$
2. $\frac{3}{4} > \frac{2}{4}$
3. $\frac{5}{6} > \frac{2}{6}$
4. $\frac{2}{3} < \frac{3}{3}$
5. $\frac{1}{4} < \frac{3}{4}$
6. $\frac{4}{5} < \frac{3}{5}$
7. $\frac{3}{8} < \frac{7}{8}$
8. $\frac{2}{3} < \frac{3}{3}$
9. $\frac{4}{5} > \frac{3}{5}$
10. $\frac{9}{10} > \frac{7}{10}$
11. $\frac{3}{4} > \frac{1}{4}$
12. $\frac{5}{8} > \frac{4}{8}$

A Great Trick

The sentences that follow the topic sentence tell more about the topic. They are called **supporting sentences**. Supporting sentences should be in an order that makes sense.

Read the topic sentence, then number the supporting ideas from 1 (first) to 4 (last).

Last week I played a great trick on my mom.

__2__ won a huge rubber snake

__1__ went to a carnival

__4__ called my mom outside

__3__ put the snake in my mom's flower garden.

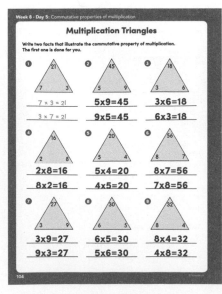

Now use the topic sentence and ideas in the correct order to write a paragraph telling the story. Be sure to use complete sentences.

Paragraph sentences will vary but should follow the same order as the numbered sentences.

Units of Measure

The side lengths of each rectangle below are labeled. Find the area of each rectangle. Make sure to label the units correctly.

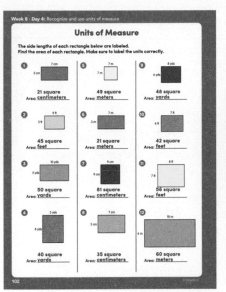

1. 7 cm × 3 cm — Area: **21 square centimeters**
2. 9 ft × 5 ft — Area: **45 square feet**
3. 10 yds × 5 yds — Area: **50 square yards**
4. 5 yds × 8 yds — Area: **40 square yards**
5. 7 m × 7 m — Area: **49 square meters**
6. 7 m × 3 m — Area: **21 square meters**
7. 9 cm × 9 cm — Area: **81 square centimeters**
8. 7 cm × 5 cm — Area: **35 square centimeters**
9. 8 yds × 6 yds — Area: **48 square yards**
10. 7 ft × 6 ft — Area: **42 square feet**
11. 8 ft × 7 ft — Area: **56 square feet**
12. 10 m × 6 m — Area: **60 square meters**

Animal Invaders

Read the articles below. Then answer the questions.

Turkey Trouble

Turkeys are popular animals around Thanksgiving. But some people in Nevada are pretty tired of them. The big birds are taking over a treasured place—Great Basin National Park.

Wild turkeys aren't native to Nevada. Ten years ago, people brought some to the area to hunt them. A few turkeys got inside the park. Their numbers began growing. Now, nearly a thousand turkeys live there.

The birds are gobbling up everything from seeds to mice. Rangers worry that this could leave less food for other animals. To stop the turkeys, they may have to trap the birds and move them to a new place.

Sniffing for Slime

Giant African snails are oozing around in Miami, Florida. The creatures are unwelcome visitors. The snails gobble up crops that people depend on for food.

African snails are an invasive species. Invasive species are plants or animals that live where they don't belong and harm native wildlife and plants. Experts say that the snails were illegally brought to the U.S. from Africa. Some escaped and quickly multiplied.

To help get rid of the snails, officials in Miami have trained dogs to locate them. The snails leave behind a stinky trail of slime that some dogs can sniff out. The furry detectives are on the hunt for thousands of snails loose in the city.

1. What main idea do the articles "Turkey Trouble" and "Sniffing for Slime" share? Cite evidence from each article that supports the main idea.

The main idea is **invasive species are causing problems in different ways.**

In "Turkey Trouble," we learn that **turkeys in Great Basin National Park are eating so much that there may not be enough for other animals.**

In "Sniffing for Slime," we find out that **snails in Miami are eating crops that humans depend on.**

2. How are officials in Nevada and Florida dealing with the problems?

In Nevada, rangers may trap the birds and move them to a new place. In Florida, officials are using dogs to find the snails.

Multiplication Triangles

Write two facts that illustrate the commutative property of multiplication. The first one is done for you.

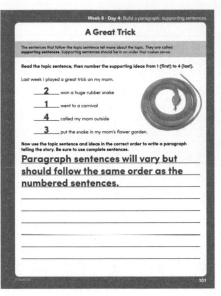

1. (21; 7, 3) $7 \times 3 = 21$; $3 \times 7 = 21$
2. (45; 5, 9) **5x9=45**; **9x5=45**
3. (18; 3, 6) **3x6=18**; **6x3=18**
4. (16; 2, 8) **2x8=16**; **8x2=16**
5. (20; 5, 4) **5x4=20**; **4x5=20**
6. (56; 8, 7) **8x7=56**; **7x8=56**
7. (27; 3, 9) **3x9=27**; **9x3=27**
8. (30; 6, 5) **6x5=30**; **5x6=30**
9. (32; 8, 4) **8x4=32**; **4x8=32**

Week 9

My Summer Vacation

Don't read the story yet! Write a word for the parts of speech listed under the blanks on the left. Then write the words in the story and read the story aloud.

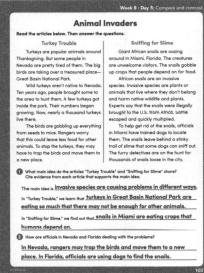

1. ________ adjective
2. ________ animal
3. ________ body part
4. ________ liquid
5. ________ plural noun
6. ________ adjective
7. ________ adjective
8. ________ adjective
9. ________ noun
10. ________ adjective
11. ________ verb ending in *-ing*
12. ________ exclamation
13. ________ number
14. ________ verb ending in *-ing*
15. ________ noun

Answers will vary.

What a ____(1)____ summer I had at Camp ____(2)____ ____(3)____! I played tricks on everyone. Once, I replaced everyone's shampoo with ____(4)____. Next, I put big ____(5)____ in their backpacks and daddy ____(6)____ legs in their food! But then the tables turned. One night after we told spooky ____(7)____ stories, I fell asleep feeling scared and ____(8)____. A sound like a loud ____(9)____ woke me. I thought I saw a ____(10)____ ghost ____(11)____ toward me! You could hear me screaming "____(12)____!" from ____(13)____ miles away! Someone turned on a flashlight, and I saw everyone ____(14)____ and laughing. The ghost was a ____(15)____ flapping in the wind. The joke was on me.

Week 9 · Day 1: Understand perimeter and area

Math's Got It Covered

Soccer players sure have a lot of ground to cover. Just how much exactly?
Answer the questions about the soccer field pictured below.
Figure out the answers in yards and then in feet.

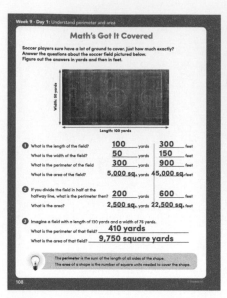

Width: 50 yards
Length: 100 yards

1. What is the length of the field? **100** yards **300** feet
   What is the width of the field? **50** yards **150** feet
   What is the perimeter of the field? **300** yards **900** feet
   What is the area of the field? **5,000 sq.** yards **45,000 sq.** feet

2. If you divide the field in half at the halfway line, what is the perimeter then? **200** yards **600** feet
   What is the area? **2,500 sq.** yards **22,500 sq.** feet

3. Imagine a field with a length of 130 yards and a width of 75 yards.
   What is the perimeter of that field? **410 yards**
   What is the area of that field? **9,750 square yards**

The perimeter is the sum of the length of all sides of the shape.
The area of a shape is the number of square units needed to cover the shape.

108

Week 9 · Day 2: Subject and object pronouns

Subject and Object Pronouns

A subject pronoun—I, you, he, she, it, they, or we—can replace the subject of a sentence.
An object pronoun—me, you, him, her, it, us, or them—can replace a noun that is the object of an action verb or that follows a preposition.

Choose the pronoun in parentheses that completes each sentence and write it on the line. Then identify the kind of pronoun it is by writing S for subject or O for object.

1. **We** ____ took a boat trip through the Everglades. (We, Us) — **S**
2. The boat's captain gave **us** ____ a special tour. (we, us) — **O**
3. The captain said, "**You** ____ will love the wildlife here!" (You, Us) — **S**
4. **I** ____ brought my camera in my backpack. (I, Me) — **S**
5. I used **it** ____ to photograph birds, turtles, and an alligator. (he, It) — **O**
6. My sister Kit carried paper and pencils with **her** ____. (she, her) — **O**
7. Kit used **them** ____ to sketch scenes of the Everglades. (they, them) — **O**
8. **She** ____ is an excellent artist. (She, Her) — **S**

Rewrite each sentence. Replace the underlined words with the correct subject or object pronoun.

9. Our grandparents sent a postcard to my sister, my brother, and me.
   They sent a postcard to us.

10. The postcard was addressed to my older brother.
    It was addressed to him.

109

Week 9 · Day 2: Fractions: parts of a whole

More Fractions

Read the fraction.
Then shade the part of the whole shape that the fraction represents.

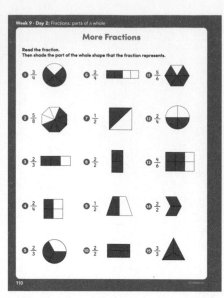

1. $\frac{3}{4}$
2. $\frac{5}{8}$
3. $\frac{2}{3}$
4. $\frac{2}{4}$
5. $\frac{2}{3}$
6. $\frac{2}{4}$
7. $\frac{1}{2}$
8. $\frac{2}{4}$
9. $\frac{1}{2}$
10. $\frac{2}{2}$
11. $\frac{5}{6}$
12. $\frac{2}{4}$
13. $\frac{4}{6}$
14. $\frac{2}{2}$
15. $\frac{3}{3}$

110

Week 9 · Day 3: Sequence

Here Comes the Sun

Do you like the sun? Here is a way to have a sun in your room every day!

You Will Need:
- a paper plate
- yellow paper
- a black pen
- yellow paint
- scissors
- a hole punch
- a brush
- a stapler
- string

Step 1: Paint the back of the plate yellow.
Step 2: Put your hand on the yellow paper. Spread your fingers. Draw around your hand. Draw your hand 7 times.
Step 3: Cut out the 7 hands.
Step 4: Staple the hands around the plate.
Step 5: Draw a happy face on your sun.
Step 6: Make a hole at the top of the plate.
Step 7: Put string through the hole. Hang up the plate in your room!

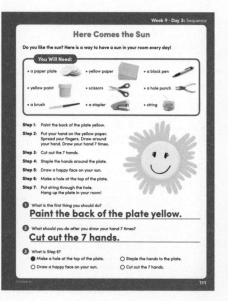

1. What is the first thing you should do?
   Paint the back of the plate yellow.

2. What should you do after you draw your hand 7 times?
   Cut out the 7 hands.

3. What is Step 6?
   ● Make a hole at the top of the plate.
   ○ Staple the hands to the plate.
   ○ Draw a happy face on your sun.
   ○ Cut out the 7 hands.

111

Week 9 · Day 3: Associative properties of multiplication

Multiplication

Rewrite each expression using the associative property.
The first two are done for you.

1. (3 x 2) x 7 — 6×7
2. 9 x (2 x 5) — 9×10
3. (3 x 2) x 5 — **6x5**
4. (4 x 2) x 6 — **8x6**
5. (2 x 5) x 7 — **10x7**
6. (3 x 2) x 6 — **6x6**
7. 9 x (3 x 3) — **9x9**
8. 6 x (2 x 5) — **6x10**
9. 7 x (4 x 2) — **7x8**
10. 4 x (4 x 2) — **4x8**
11. (2 x 4) x 6 — **8x6**
12. (2 x 2) x 8 — **4x8**
13. (2 x 2) x 9 — **4x9**
14. (3 x 3) x 7 — **9x7**
15. (2 x 3) x 9 — **6x9**

112

Week 9 · Day 4: Combine sentences

Great Gardening Tips

Sentences can be combined to make them more interesting.
Key words can help put two sentences together. For example:
Old: I will plan my garden. I am waiting for spring.
New: I will plan my garden while I am waiting for spring.

Write a new sentence using the key words in each flower.

1. Fill a cup with water. Add some flower seeds. **and**
   Fill a cup with water and add some flower seeds.

2. Let them soak. They need to be softened. **because**
   Let them soak because they need to be softened.

3. Fill a cup with dirt. The seeds soak in water. **while**
   Fill a cup with dirt while the seeds soak in water.

4. Bury the seeds in the cup. The dirt covers them. **until**
   Bury the seeds in the cup until the dirt covers them.

5. Add water to the plant. Do not add too much water. **but**
   Add water to the plant but do not add too much water.

6. Set the cup in the sun. The plant will grow. **so**
   Set the cup in the sun so the plant will grow.

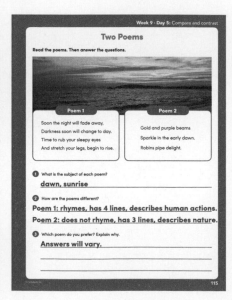

113

Week 9 · Day 4: Identify fractions on a number line

Fractions on a Number Line

Label the fractions on each number line. The first one is done for you.

1. 0 $\frac{1}{8}$ $\frac{2}{8}$ $\frac{3}{8}$ $\frac{4}{8}$ $\frac{5}{8}$ $\frac{6}{8}$ $\frac{7}{8}$ 1
2. 0 $\frac{1}{5}$ $\frac{2}{5}$ $\frac{3}{5}$ $\frac{4}{5}$ 1
3. 0 $\frac{1}{12}$ $\frac{2}{12}$ $\frac{3}{12}$ $\frac{4}{12}$ $\frac{5}{12}$ $\frac{6}{12}$ $\frac{7}{12}$ $\frac{8}{12}$ $\frac{9}{12}$ $\frac{10}{12}$ $\frac{11}{12}$ 1
4. 0 $\frac{1}{6}$ $\frac{2}{6}$ $\frac{3}{6}$ $\frac{4}{6}$ $\frac{5}{6}$ 1
5. 0 $\frac{1}{2}$ 1
6. 0 $\frac{1}{7}$ $\frac{2}{7}$ $\frac{3}{7}$ $\frac{4}{7}$ $\frac{5}{7}$ $\frac{6}{7}$ 1
7. 0 $\frac{1}{4}$ $\frac{2}{4}$ $\frac{3}{4}$ 1
8. 0 $\frac{1}{3}$ $\frac{2}{3}$ 1
9. 0 $\frac{1}{10}$ $\frac{2}{10}$ $\frac{3}{10}$ $\frac{4}{10}$ $\frac{5}{10}$ $\frac{6}{10}$ $\frac{7}{10}$ $\frac{8}{10}$ $\frac{9}{10}$ 1

114

Week 9 · Day 5: Compare and contrast

Two Poems

Read the poems. Then answer the questions.

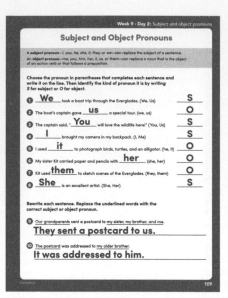

Poem 1
Soon the night will fade away,
Darkness soon will change to day.
Time to rub your sleepy eyes
And stretch your legs, begin to rise.

Poem 2
Gold and purple beams
Sparkle in the early dawn.
Robins pipe delight.

1. What is the subject of each poem?
   dawn, sunrise

2. How are the poems different?
   Poem 1: rhymes, has 4 lines, describes human actions.
   Poem 2: does not rhyme, has 3 lines, describes nature.

3. Which poem do you prefer? Explain why.
   Answers will vary.

115

Week 9 · Day 5: Multiplication and division fact families

Flying With Fact Families

Write the multiplication and division sentences for each set of numbers.

The fact family for 5, 6, and 30 is:
5 x 6 = 30   30 ÷ 6 = 5
6 x 5 = 30   30 ÷ 5 = 6

1. 2, 3, 6
   2x3=6
   3x2=6
   6÷2=3
   6÷3=2

2. 3, 7, 21
   3x7=21
   7x3=21
   21÷3=7
   21÷7=3

3. 3, 6, 18
   3x6=18
   6x3=18
   18÷3=6
   18÷6=3

4. 6, 7, 42
   6x7=42
   7x6=42
   42÷6=7
   42÷7=6

5. 7, 8, 56
   7x8=56
   8x7=56
   56÷7=8
   56÷8=7

6. 6, 9, 54
   6x9=54
   9x6=54
   54÷6=9
   54÷9=6

7. 5, 12, 60
   5x12=60
   12x5=60
   60÷5=12
   60÷12=5

8. 8, 9, 72
   8x9=72
   9x8=72
   72÷8=9
   72÷9=8

9. 9, 12, 108
   9x12=108
   12x9=108
   108÷9=12
   108÷12=9

10. 11, 12, 132
    11x12=132
    12x11=132
    132÷11=12
    132÷12=11

11. 4, 5, 20
    4x5=20
    5x4=20
    20÷4=5
    20÷5=4

12. 5, 7, 35
    5x7=35
    7x5=35
    35÷5=7
    35÷7=5

Challenge — **24÷4=6 members**
There are 4 families traveling together on an airplane. They need 24 seats in all.
If each family has the same number of members, how many are in each family?

116

Week 10

Look Who's Talking

Quotation marks surround a character's exact words. In a statement, use a comma to separate the character's exact words from the rest of the sentence. In a question and an exclamation, use the correct ending punctuation after the character's exact words.

Statement: *"I have to go now," said my friend.*
Question: *"Where are you?" asked my mom.*
Exclamation: *"Wow!" the boy exclaimed.*

Look at the pictures and read the speech bubbles below. Place what each child says in a sentence. Use quotation marks and correct punctuation. The above examples can help you.

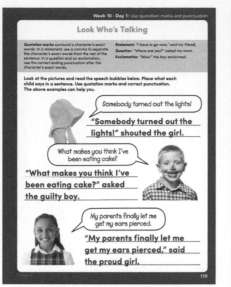

Somebody turned out the lights!

"Somebody turned out the lights!" shouted the girl.

What makes you think I've been eating cake?

"What makes you think I've been eating cake?" asked the guilty boy.

My parents finally let me get my ears pierced.

"My parents finally let me get my ears pierced," said the proud girl.

119

Decision Time

Decide whether to multiply or divide. Solve.

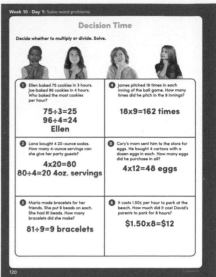

1 Ellen baked 75 cookies in 3 hours. Joe baked 96 cookies in 4 hours. Who baked the most cookies per hour?

$75 \div 3 = 25$
$96 \div 4 = 24$
Ellen

2 Lana made 4 20-ounce sodas. How many 4-ounce servings can she give her party guests?

$4 \times 20 = 80$
$80 \div 4 = 20$ **4oz. servings**

3 Maria made bracelets for her friends. She put 9 beads on each. She had 81 beads. How many bracelets did she make?

$81 \div 9 = 9$ **bracelets**

4 James pitched 18 times in each inning of the ball game. How many times did he pitch in the 9 innings?

$18 \times 9 = 162$ **times**

5 Cory's mom sent him to the store for eggs. He bought 4 cartons with a dozen eggs in each. How many eggs did he purchase in all?

$4 \times 12 = 48$ **eggs**

6 It costs 1.50¢ per hour to park at the beach. How much did it cost David's parents to park for 8 hours?

$\$1.50 \times 8 = \$12$

120

Attack of the Massive Watermelon!

Don't read the story yet! Write a word for the parts of speech listed under the blanks on the left. Then write the words in the story and read the story aloud.

Answers will vary.

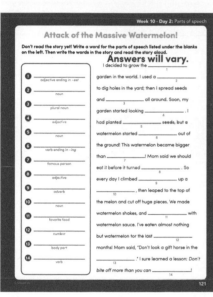

1. adjective ending in -est
2. noun
3. plural noun
4. adjective
5. noun
6. verb ending in -ing
7. famous person
8. adjective
9. adverb
10. noun
11. favorite food
12. number
13. body part
14. verb

I decided to grow the _____ garden in the world. I used a _____ to dig holes in the yard; then I spread seeds and _____ all around. Soon, my garden started looking _____. I had planted _____ seeds, but a watermelon started _____ out of the ground! This watermelon became bigger than _____! Mom said we should eat it before it turned _____. So every day I climbed _____ up a _____, then leaped to the top of the melon and cut off huge pieces. We made watermelon shakes, and _____ with watermelon sauce. I've eaten almost nothing but watermelon for the last _____ months! Mom said, "Don't look a gift horse in the _____! I sure learned a lesson: Don't bite off more than you can _____.

121

Mr. Knapp's Rug Shop

The **perimeter** is the distance around a figure. To find the perimeter, add together the length of the two sides and the width of the two sides.
The **area** of a figure is the number of square units inside a figure. The area of a figure can be found by multiplying the length times the width.

Mr. Knapp's rugs are too plain! Follow the directions below and help him by making his rugs much more attractive.

- Draw flowers on the rug with a perimeter of 26 feet.
- Draw stripes on the rug with a perimeter of 20 feet.
- Draw a smiling face in the center of the rug with an area of 36 feet.
- Draw a design of your choice on the rug with an area of 15 feet.

Check your child's drawings.

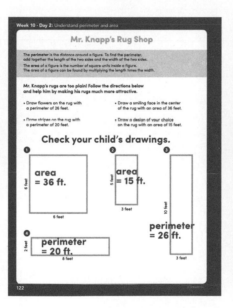

1 6 feet / 6 feet — area = 36 ft.

2 5 feet / 3 feet — area = 15 ft.

3 10 feet / 3 feet — perimeter = 26 ft.

4 2 feet / 8 feet — perimeter = 20 ft.

122

Sequence Words

Sequence is the order in which events happen. Words such as *now, then, when, soon, next, later, while, before,* and *after* help explain when an event happened in relation to another event. Writers use sequence words to make their writing clear to readers.

Underline the sequence words in each sentence.

1 **Before** we went to the party, we wrapped our gifts.
2 **When** we arrived, we saw all the beautiful decorations.
3 **After** greeting our host, we put our gifts on the table.
4 **Soon**, other guests began to arrive.
5 **While** Joe opened his gifts, the guests were served cake and soda.
6 **After**, a comedian told jokes.
7 **Finally**, it was time to leave.
8 **Now**, we can just go home.

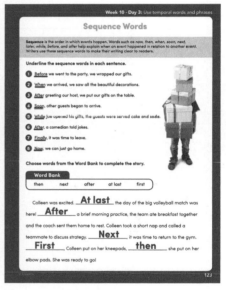

Choose words from the Word Bank to complete the story.

Word Bank
then   next   after   at last   first

Colleen was excited. **At last** the day of the big volleyball match was here! **After** a brief morning practice, the team ate breakfast together and the coach sent them home to rest. Colleen took a short nap and called a teammate to discuss strategy. **Next** it was time to return to the gym. **First** Colleen put on her kneepads, **then** she put on her elbow pads. She was ready to go!

123

Equal Fractions

Two equal fractions are shown on each pair of number lines. Write the equal fractions above the number lines. The first one is done for you.

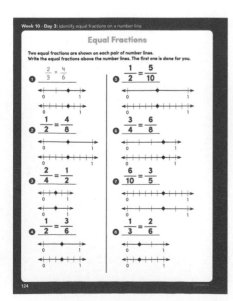

1 $\frac{2}{3} = \frac{4}{6}$

2 $\frac{2}{4} = \frac{4}{8}$

3 $\frac{2}{4} = \frac{1}{2}$

4 $\frac{2}{6} = \frac{1}{3}$

5 $\frac{1}{2} = \frac{5}{10}$

6 $\frac{3}{4} = \frac{6}{8}$

7 $\frac{6}{10} = \frac{3}{5}$

8 $\frac{1}{2} = \frac{2}{4}$

124

Closing Time!

The last sentence in a paragraph is called the **closing sentence**. It restates the topic sentence in a new way.

Find a closing sentence to match each topic sentence. Write the closing sentence.

Closing Sentences
Some gardeners in Florida and Texas can enjoy their flowers all year long.
Of all the seasons, autumn is the best.
Life would never be the same without computers.
There are many subjects in school, but math is the most difficult.
Though dangerous, the job of an astronaut is exciting.

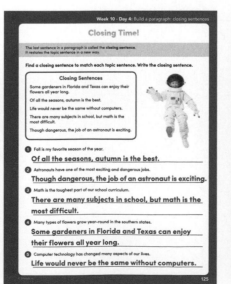

1 Fall is my favorite season of the year.
Of all the seasons, autumn is the best.

2 Astronauts have one of the most exciting and dangerous jobs.
Though dangerous, the job of an astronaut is exciting.

3 Math is the toughest part of our school curriculum.
There are many subjects in school, but math is the most difficult.

4 Many types of flowers grow year-round in the southern states.
Some gardeners in Florida and Texas can enjoy their flowers all year long.

5 Computer technology has changed many aspects of our lives.
Life would never be the same without computers.

125

Quick Dry

Engineer David Hu wanted to determine how different mammals shake to dry off. He found that the smaller the animal, the faster it shook. He measured both the animals' shaking rates and the radius of their torsos (measured from behind the animal's shoulders). Hu found that there was a relationship between the animals' torso radius and the speed at which they shook.

Use the data in the chart about the animals' torso sizes to complete the blank bar graph. Make sure you give your graph a title and label the vertical and horizontal axes. Then answer the questions that follow.

Animal Torso Sizes	
Animal	Radius (centimeters)
Brown bear	24
Gulf Coast sheep	15
Kangaroo	8.1
Kunekune pig	13.3
Rat	2.6
River otter	5.5

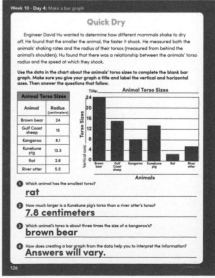

Title: **Animal Torso Sizes**

1 Which animal has the smallest torso?
rat

2 How much larger is a Kunekune pig's torso than a river otter's torso?
7.8 centimeters

3 Which animal's torso is about three times the size of a kangaroo's?
brown bear

4 How does creating a bar graph from the data help you to interpret the information?
Answers will vary.

126

141

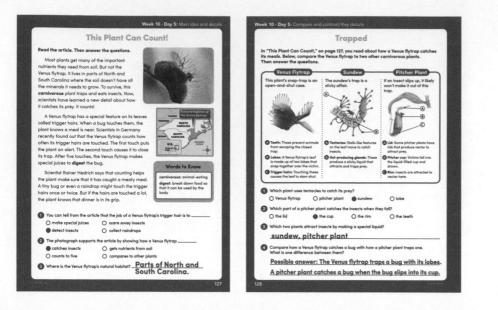

This Plant Can Count!

Read the article. Then answer the questions.

Most plants get many of the important nutrients they need from soil. But not the Venus flytrap. It lives in parts of North and South Carolina where the soil doesn't have all the minerals it needs to grow. To survive, this **carnivorous** plant traps and eats insects. Now, scientists have learned a new detail about how it catches its prey. It counts!

A Venus flytrap has a special feature on its leaves called trigger hairs. When a bug touches them, the plant knows a meal is near. Scientists in Germany recently found out that the Venus flytrap counts how often its trigger hairs are touched. The first touch puts the plant on alert. The second touch causes it to close its trap. After five touches, the Venus flytrap makes special juices to **digest** the bug.

Scientist Rainer Hedrich says that counting helps the plant make sure that it has caught a meaty meal. A tiny bug or even a raindrop might touch the trigger hairs once or twice. But if the hairs are touched a lot, the plant knows that dinner is in its grip.

natural habitat of the Venus flytrap

Words to Know

carnivorous: animal-eating
digest: break down food so that it can be used by the body

1 You can tell from the article that the job of a Venus flytrap's trigger hair is to _____
- ○ make special juices
- ● detect insects
- ○ scare away insects
- ○ collect raindrops

2 The photograph supports the article by showing how a Venus flytrap _____
- ● catches insects
- ○ counts to five
- ○ gets nutrients from soil
- ○ compares to other plants

3 Where is the Venus flytrap's natural habitat? **Parts of North and South Carolina.**

127

Trapped

In "This Plant Can Count!," on page 127, you read about how a Venus flytrap catches its meals. Below, compare the Venus flytrap to two other carnivorous plants. Then answer the questions.

Venus Flytrap	Sundew	Pitcher Plant
This plant's snap-trap is an open-and-shut case.	The sundew's trap is a sticky affair.	If an insect slips up, it likely won't make it out of this trap.

Venus Flytrap
- **A Teeth:** These prevent animals from escaping the closed trap.
- **B Lobes:** A Venus flytrap's leaf is made up of two lobes that snap together over the victim.
- **C Trigger hairs:** Touching these causes the leaf to slam shut.

Sundew
- **A Tentacles:** Stalk-like features on the leaf move to catch insects.
- **B Gel-producing glands:** These produce a sticky liquid that attracts and traps prey.

Pitcher Plant
- **A Lid:** Some pitcher plants have lids that produce nectar to attract prey.
- **B Pitcher cup:** Victims fall into the liquid-filled cup and drown.
- **C Rim:** Insects are attracted to nectar here.

1 Which plant uses tentacles to catch its prey?
- ○ Venus flytrap
- ○ pitcher plant
- ● sundew
- ○ lobe

2 Which part of a pitcher plant catches the insects when they fall?
- ○ the lid
- ● the cup
- ○ the rim
- ○ the teeth

3 Which two plants attract insects by making a special liquid?
sundew, pitcher plant

4 Compare how a Venus flytrap catches a bug with how a pitcher plant traps one. What is one difference between them?
Possible answer: The Venus flytrap traps a bug with its lobes. A pitcher plant catches a bug when the bug slips into its cup.

128

FOR OUTSTANDING ACHIEVEMENT

CONGRATULATIONS!

This certificate is awarded to

I'm proud of you!